TOOLS FOR POLICY ANALYSIS AND MANAGEMENT

A PRACTIONER'S GUIDE

Bonard Mwape

authorHOUSE®

AuthorHouse™ UK
1663 Liberty Drive
Bloomington, IN 47403 USA
www.authorhouse.co.uk
Phone: 0800.197.4150

Published by AuthorHouse 07/19/2018

ISBN: 978-1-5462-9047-6 (sc)
ISBN: 978-1-5462-9046-9 (e)

Library of Congress Control Number: 2018908087

Print information available on the last page.

This book is printed on acid-free paper.

CONTENTS

LIST OF FIGURES

LIST OF TABLES

ACKNOWLEDGMENTS

We have had significant help in making this book a reality. Students from our various MBA classes in Tanzania, Zambia, Kenya, Uganda, Malawi, Zimbabwe, Swaziland, Namibia, and Seychelles gave a unique environment in, which to create the required topics and to have a book with tools that could improve management decision making.

Our students from these campuses contributed to the ideas in this book. They did help us reflect upon our ideas and offered valuable comments and support. Our ESAMI faculty who teach policy analysis gave some ideas in this book, which they have used to our executive and MBA students, which provide us with valuable information that sharpened our thinking about policy analysis.

During the course of our teaching and research on policy analysis, we have met with corporate executives and public officers around the continent who thought that policy analysis is not a concern only for public or governmental agencies but also takes place in business organizations.

We would like also to thank many MBA students, whose class exercises have been used to enrich this book. Thanks also to Peter Kiuluku and Sandy Banda for their wise comments and editorial feedback.

Finally, appreciation goes to my wife, Judith, for originating the idea of having a book that brings together tools in policy analysis, tools that may be used by any manager both in the public and private sector. As an entrepreneur she knew why tools to increase creativity were important in business. Thank you so much.

Finally, to my children who were always for me. They wanted me to rest but also complete the book.

PREFACE

Anyone involved in the policy process analyzes policy in some sense. However, those who analyze and manage public policy professionally must use a variety of tools to do their job effectively. This book, *Tools for Policy Analysis and Management*, discusses topics and presents tools and methodologies central to the tasks of policy analysis and management. The general approach and the specific suggestions made have been developed over many years of teaching policy analysis to graduate students as well as executive education workshops for policymakers and analysts.

Providing advice to key decision makers is scary, but it is also exhilarating. Policy analysts have to "speak truth to power." In order to do this effectively, they need analytical skill as well as the policy analysis tools. You will find in the pages of this book the analytical tools that will empower policy analysts to do their job well.

Policies are instruments for solving real-life problems within adaptive systems such as societies and governments. Uncertainty, ambiguity and disagreements surround the arena for policy analysis and management. In such an environment, how is the future forecast and explored? How are policy problems identified, conceptualized, and structured? How are policy stakeholders identified, analyzed, and managed? How are policy options identified and recommendations made? How is the truth actually told to power? How are policies monitored and evaluated so that policymakers will be able to provide meaningful evidence in support of any claims they might wish to make about a policy's effectiveness? *Tools for Policy Analysis and Management* provides the policy analysis tools and their application in dealing with these and more questions.

My goal for writing this book is to empower policy analysts to provide comprehensive and persuasive argument justifying their policy recommendations to decision makers and leaders. This is because at the end of the day, leaders (elected or appointed) have to make decisions. If policy analysts do not know the answers or lack the information they need, they are going to make decisions anyway. However, different policy decisions on the same policy problem may create different futures with different outcomes. It is imperative for policy analysts to explore these futures in advance of the decision by asking the right questions. This is the heart of good policy analysis.

This book helps you to explore the right policy analysis tools.

I have organized this book around the various stages in the policy making process for the public sector, which include problem identification, policy formulation, policy implementation, policy adoption, and policy evaluation. The first three chapters present the conceptual foundation of a policy, highlighting the sources of policy problems and the management of the policy process. Chapters 4 to 10 discuss the various analytical tools and methods used at each stage of the policy making process. Practical examples are presented to demonstrate the application of the tools and methods discussed. The last chapter is dedicated to the writing of policy papers and several examples and templates of policy papers are presented.

The presumed user is a practitioner preparing to undertake a policy analysis. However, this book is also useful at both ends of the spectrum— in teaching graduate students' public policy courses as well as executive education for policymakers and analysts.

My hope is that this publication, *Tools of Policy Analysis and Management*, will help policy analysts apply the concepts, tools, and methods it contains. The result is to deepen the knowledge base on which policies are designed and analyzed so as to enhance decision making by the centers of power.

CHAPTER 1

Conceptual Foundation of a Policy

This chapter presents some key concepts used in policy formulation analysis and management.

1.1 What Is a Policy?

The word *policy* comes from several backgrounds. Dunn (1984) says the nearest to the word came from the Greek and Latin languages. In the Greek language, the word *polis* means "city-state"; in Latin, *politia* also means "state." During the Middle Ages, the English word *policy* appeared, while in Germanic and Slavic languages, the word appeared as *politick* or *politika*. Hence, in the beginning, *politika* sounds like *policy*, but then these words had meanings other than "policy" (Dunn 1984).

1.2 Variety of Definitions of the Word

In the most recent times, especially since World War II, usage of the word *policy* shows there are a number of ways it is used. However, if we group these definitions, two conceptual limbs emerge. These are the traditional problem solving approaches, also referred to as the linear model approach and the process models.

1.3 The Linear Model Approach

The traditional approach to policy defines policy as "the implicit or explicit specification of courses of purposive action being followed or to be followed in dealing with a recognized problem or matter of concern and directed toward the accomplishment of some intended or desired set of goals" (Harman 1984). Jennings (1977) had the same view when he said, "Policy is a guide for taking future actions and for making appropriate choices or decisions toward the accomplishment of some intended or desired end. By policy we mean 'what an organization chooses to do or not to do'" (Dye 1972). For others "a policy is a set of interrelated decisions taken concerning the selection of goals and means of achieving them" (Jenkins 1976) or "a purposive course of action dealing with a problem or a matter of concern" (Anderson 1984). For Gallagher, policy takes a legalistic dimension when she defines policy as "a formal act, that has an agreed-upon intent, is sanctioned or approved by an institutional body or authority, and provides a consistent standard for measuring performance" (Gallagher 1992).

Accordingly, in the traditional sense, policy "is a set of instructions from policy makers to policy implementers that spell out both goals and the means for achieving those goals" (Nudzor 2009). This rationalist approach to policy reveals a technocratic approach to policy and policy making in general (Dunn 1984). It portrays policy making as involving "a group of authorized decision makers [who] assemble at particular times and places, review a problem ... [c]onsider a number of alternative courses of action with more or less explicit calculation of the advantages and disadvantages of each option, weigh the alternatives against their goals or preferences, and then select an alternative that seems well suited for achieving their purposes. The result is a decision" (Weiss 1982).

1.4 Practical Use of Rational Approach

Policy is used to denote an event and or an act of setting out solutions to problems. The paradigm takes policy analysis as a rational process. Policy process is taken to be a process of searching for a solution in a certain problem space. It presumes first, that policy analysts are experts who have proper analytical techniques. They—policy analysts—apply policy analysis as a rational activity that follows rational stages (Shulock 1999). In this approach, policy analysts need to have complete information about the initial state of the task/problem and then move from problem state to solutions.

In another form of usage, the rationalistic approach describes policy as a statement of prescribed intent and an authoritative allocation of values (Kogan 1975). It involves the implicit or explicit specification of courses of purposive action to be followed or already being followed in dealing with a recognized problem or matter of concern (Herman 1984). In this case, policy is a positivist stance developed in response to a problem. Policy is a product of the decision making process encapsulated in a document indicating statements of intention or of practice as perceived by policy actors (Jennings 1977).

To be seen as effective, policy analysts must first have the capacity to discover and measure the impact of policy on the organization and its stakeholders. Second, policy analysts must project policy consequences with accuracy (Descomb 2002). Third, policy analysts must know the stages of rational problem solving.

1.5 The Policy Process Approach

The problem solving and rational approach to policy has come under criticism, especially from the "policy circle" conception of policy analysis (Bowe et al. 1992; Vidovich 2001). They have worked with a process conceptualization of policy. They see policy making as a multidimensional and multifaceted process (Hope 2009), "which evolves through cycles more or less bounded or less constrained by time, funds, political support and other events. It is also a process that circles back on itself, iterates the same decision issue time and again and often does not come to closure" (Rist 2000; Vidovich 2001).

A policy then, according to process models, is seen as being complex. Policy Texts are seen as products of compromise and contestations (Ball 1994).

In this regard, if policy is contested and often a product of negotiations, policies shift. There are real struggles, disputes, conflicts and adjustments in the policy process. (Ball 1994).

This so-called postmodernist way of looking at policy presents it as a complex and contested process rather than an end.

1.6 Use of Policy Process Ideas

All policy process approaches recognize a multi-actor setting of policy problems, the divergence of perceptions, and the need for interaction and communication to solve problems (Edelenbos 2003).

In this regard, because of a complex unstructured problem, setting a purely content-directed approach is not seen to be possible (De Bruijin 2002). In this approach, for policy analysts to be successful in their work, they must first know all actors, as the latter are the focal point of the analysis. Second, the approach assumes policy problems and solutions are only relevant to the policy process if they are presented by an actor. However, this way of thinking excludes policy solutions that come from within the institutions. It also does not tell us how the "un organized and " passive masses' ideas enter the policy process. Third, we know that policy formulation does not come from an intended course of action formulated by one actor but results from a series of decisions made by different actors in different rounds of interaction. Fourth, the rounds of decision-making are only determined by the policy analyst in retrospect by discerning the most crucial decisions. Hence, one notes that decision making rounds are characterized by dynamic combinations of sets of problems and solutions as presented by different actors (Kopper and Kliyn 2004) within and outside the policy process.

1.7 The Tools for Success

In policy process approaches, for policy analysts to add value to the decision making process, formulating a problem and its solution implies that uncertainty, ambiguity, and disagreements need to be reduced. Stakeholders' perceptions and knowledge are taken to be central elements in order to create a joint problem formulation. The skill is to know that the outcome of problem structuring is negotiated knowledge (Van de Riet 2003).

The policy process appears dynamic by introducing the thinking that policy is not an end but a means for not politicians alone but even people from outside. It also emphasizes a bottom-up approach to policy making as compared to the traditional centralist approach.

Despite this contribution, the process approach has its own weakness, which lies in its overemphasis on the discretion of the micro actors of policy but fails to recognize the fact that it is the macro level actors that set the ground rules (Trowler 1998). Similarly, the process approaches by focusing on the process and actors. The model does not tell us what the policy is. Rather, it indicates how actors respond to the policy.

Therefore, in understanding the role of a policy analyst in the policy process, we need an eclectic view of the two approaches. This is because whether policy is conceptualized as a course of action to be followed or a process involving discourse and contestations, overlaps exist between these two approaches. The practical way to understand policy is to take policy as "both that, which is thought of and positioned to alter an existing situation [and that] which is struggled or contested over within the policy terrain" (Niedzor 2009).

Hence, the policy analyst must know that policy is what is intentionally made and set to rectify an issue of concern as well as what is enacted and/or struggled over within the policy terrain. Thus, when participating in the policy process, the policy analyst must often speak truth to power. How the policy will be conceived, conceptualized, and operationalized would, in most cases, depend on the interpretive work of the policy analyst as influenced by the discursive context within, which the policy takes place (Ozga 2000).

1.8 Practical Use of Policy

A most useful and practical way of defining a policy is provided by William Dunn (1984). Dunn defines policies as guidelines formulated or adopted by an organization to reach its long-term goals so that all major decisions, actions, and activities take place within the boundaries set by those prolonged policies. This definition takes policies not as technical instruments but as a body of principles that underpin the operations of an organization. Therefore, policies must reflect the organization's value system. This means policies are the state of affairs we prepare. They define the character of the organization, while to 'work with' means policies are boundaries for acceptable or unacceptable behaviors. They are instruments we use to achieve our visions, while our missions (what we do here) define policy boundaries.

Since they are instruments and value systems, policies regulate organization behavior and reinforce existing social expectations or encourage constructive change. Hence, a good policy should be considered as a statement of intent or a commitment. When they are commitments, for that reason at least, decision makers can be held accountable for the policies they formulate and popularize.

At the second level, a policy can be a course of action to guide and influence decisions. Once approved or made, it can guide decision making under a given set of circumstances within the framework of objectives and goals as determined by the organization.

1.9 The Difference between Policies and Procedures

A policy is a *guiding principle* used to set direction in an organization, while a procedure is a *series of steps to be followed* as a consistent and repetitive approach to accomplish a result set by policy. Together; policies and procedures are used to empower the people responsible for a process with the direction and consistency they need for successful *process improvement.*

1.9.1 "Why Do We Need Policies and Procedures?"

The purpose of having policies and procedures is to have an internal control system. By defining and documenting policies with well-written procedures, we enhance

- compliance;

- operational efficiency;

- risk management; and

- continuous improvement.

Linkage between Policy, Procedures, Rules and Laws.

A policy guideline is a specific series of actions or operations, which have to be executed in the same manner in order to always obtain the same result under the same circumstances. Procedures are sequences of tasks or steps taken to achieve the results. Rules or laws provide boundaries within, which right or wrong is determined.

1.10 What Is the Role of a Policy?

The general role of a policy is to provide direction and guide decisions and actions in a particular area (Smith 2002). Often policies are used to avoid negative consequences and to produce effects that are useful and positive to stakeholders. That is why a policy is considered as a "Statement of Intent" or a "Commitment." The OECD (2000) argues that a policy is not a panacea in itself. It is an important factor that guides action toward achieving a certain objective. Policies are normative because they are mechanisms through, which values are authoritatively allocated in a society or organization. However, we can identify specific contributions of policy in the management of the organization. Namely:

1.10.1 Policies Provide Objective Reasoning as follows:

Decision making is a process of selecting a course of action which forms the basis for a common course of action.

1. Successful managers ensure that there is consistency in choices or decisions; (If the problem definition is the same, decision choices; are always kept the same),

2. Those same standards are applied to all members of staff and to all problems that the organization has defined. This leads to objectivity in decision making.

1.10.2 Policies Provide Confident Decision Making

- For the system to bring confidence in the decision making machinery, it is imperative that a set of policies on significant issues are drawn and applied for reference.

- As long as the problem definition on the ground is similar or identical to the problem definition that is in the policy framework, managers must adopt the policy choice, and that becomes a binding decision. This brings staff more confidence in the decision making system than applying different criteria on similar problems.

1.10.3 Policies Provide Reliable Reference Framework

- The produced policy manual in the organization will be a guide on the type of choices to be made when certain types of problems have been defined.

1.10.4 Policies Provide Transparency

- Transparency in decision making is vital and key to gaining employee support and acceptance. This is because if employees trust the decision making machinery, they tend to own the decision.

- The process to transparent decision making starts with the policy formulation procedures. If stakeholders are allowed to participate and give input, the results are likely to be representative and generally acceptable. This is because employees will know what decisions will be taken even before they go to their managers for opinions. Indeed, transparent policies are what build a strong culture of success in organizations, and this better ensures success in meeting an organization's goals.

1.10.5 Policies Enable Speedy Decision

- It is undisputable that a properly drafted policy framework not only solves problems but also saves everybody's time so that everybody is able to concentrate on other value-adding courses of action.

- With policies in place, managers only have to check if the problem is covered in policies and then apply the policy choices for a solution.

1.10.6 Policies Enable Accountability

- Policies are used for accountability and answerability

- Effective delegation is about policy centers, which ensures that each center works according to the policy results.

1.10.7 Policies as Future Anticipators

- Policies take and present past and present problem definition. We must understand, however, that the policy is going to be used in the future. Hence good Policies must be proactive and tailored to generally guiding all future actions.

1.10.8 Policies Are Organization Culture Builders

- Policies shape corporate behavior to a certain expected way of doing things. Policies achieve this by looking at the objectives of the organization and accordingly manage risks, which might prevent achievement of these objectives.

1.10.9 Policies and Quality Decisions

- Business survives on decisions. Successful organizations have boasted of decisions, which are able to respond to customer needs as and when those needs can be discerned or anticipated. Businesses, which fail lose out to competition through a series of poor decisions. Failure is therefore either an issue of goal incongruence or a case of suboptimization. Whatever the reason, the fact is that such a business has failed to manage the present and the future. For there to be success, decisions are supposed to be aligned to the success levels of the organization. Hence, decision makers must ensure that before decisions are taken, they know exactly whether the impact of their decisions will achieve the goals of the organization.

1.11 Policy Framework

- In most cases the policy framework helps identify essential large policy areas as well as particular activities in each area. Therefore, policy frameworks constitute strategic management decision zones that help simplify complex policy issues in manageable and similar policy goals.

Figure 1: Illustration of a Policy Framework

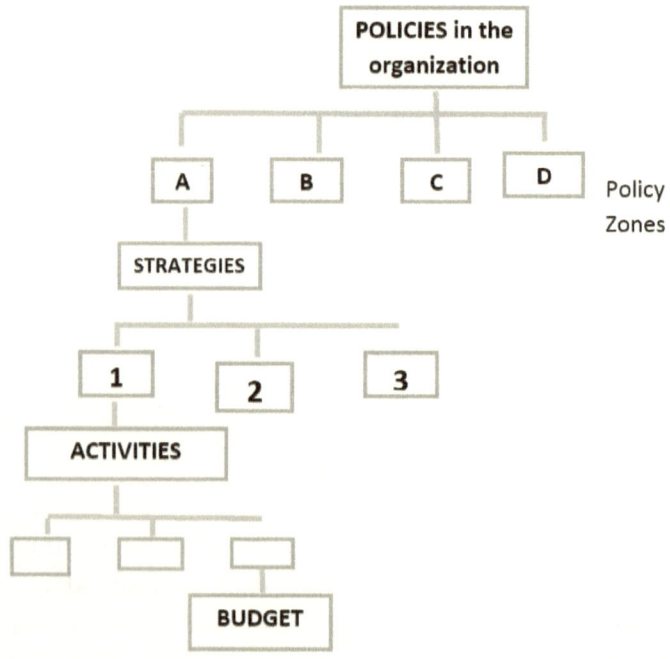

Types of Policies

The organization normally has three broad policy Instruments. *Internal policies* deal with staff and their interaction with their organization. Such policies deal with staff promotion, discipline, training, recruitment, etc., and all those provide the guidelines on what are acceptable and unacceptable practices. These policies enable the employee to have a reference framework for objective decision making.

Interactive policies, on the other hand, provide guidelines to employees in their day-to-day interactions with customers, i.e., the outside world.

External policies present the organization to the outside world.

Figure 2: Types of Policies

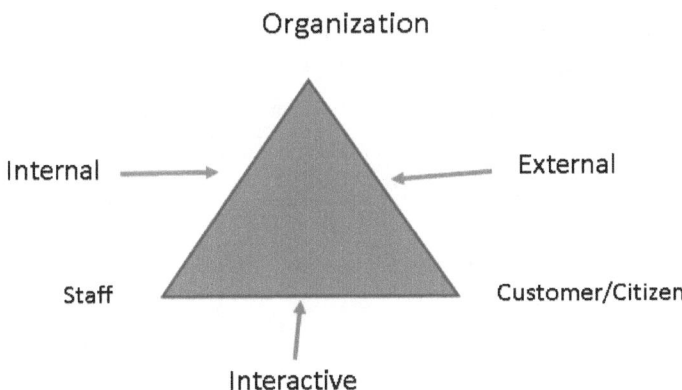

1.12 Policy Levels

There are several policy levels in any organization. Policy levels reflect policy domains. Most organizations have governance, strategic, and operational policy domains.

- The governance policy domain consists of high level policies, which articulate principles that instruct management across key strategic areas of the organization. The governance policies are

11

usually approved by the board or highest policy making body and apply across the organization.

- Strategic and operational policies tend to be lower-order policies, which translate the governance level into strategic action.

1.13 The Policy Value Chain

Effective and efficient operations require policy alignment of both high- and low-level policies, which form policy value chains across the organization. High-level policies govern the entire organization in most or all circumstances. They speak of company desires, needs, and aspirations. High-level policy doesn't readily lend itself to procedures; instead, it takes the form of a standard or a general guideline.

A low-level policy chain deals with a more specific set of circumstances. Low-level policy is the kind that usually leads to procedures. An example of a low-level policy that everyone is familiar with has to do with attendance. For example, employees are expected to come to the office to carry out their duties during "normal working hours." This sentence in many African organizations translates into 0800 to 1700 hours.

The challenge with policy chains is how to continually change them to fit the rapidly changing global environment.

1.14 Policy Effects

Policies frequently have side effects or unintended consequences. This is because the environments that policies seek to influence or manipulate are complex adaptive systems, and making a policy change can have counterintuitive results. For example, a government may make a policy decision to raise taxes, with hopes of increasing overall tax revenue. Depending on the size of the tax increase, this may have the overall effect of reducing tax revenue by causing capital flight; alternatively, high tax rates may deter some citizens from earning the money subject to such taxes.

The policy formulation process typically includes an attempt to assess as many areas of potential policy impact as possible, to lessen the chances that a given policy will have unexpected or unintended consequences. [1]However, because of the nature of complex adaptive systems such as societies and governments, it may sometimes be difficult to assess all possible impacts of a given policy. Hence policy effectiveness requires continuous learning on the performance of the introduced policies to be able to align our initiatives.

---

[1]   https://en.wikipedia.org/wiki/Policy

CHAPTER 2

Designing a Policy

2.1 Where Do Policy Problems Come From?

Several schools of thought exist dealing with how and where policy agendas come from and how they enter the policy process. Here we present some of the most influential approaches.

2.1.1 Positivist/Elitist Arguments

Dunn's policy agenda framework provides a policy process that can be seen to be positivist. He argues that once an idea enters public discussion, it must eventually come out as an Institutional agenda. An Institutional agenda by the same token will be turned into a policy by the relevant organization. In this approach the role of the policy analyst is to follow agendas and then generate policy issues and evidence to push forward private agendas to institutional agendas. Where necessary the policy analyst should commission studies to elaborate on the said issues and refine them to come up with organization policy solutions (Dunn 1981).

Of course what one sees in this approach is a possibility that some issues may die unless they are pushed along. Therefore, the policy analyst may be seen to play both the role of an expert adviser and also a champion of ideas as issues move from public agenda to institutional agenda.

Dunn provides a method that presents the policy process as if it is dominantly or exclusively expert driven. That is why Robert Entman 1977) tried to modify Dunn's approval based on the closed system approach by emphasizing the influence of the public opinion and policy narratives in agenda transformation.

Entman discussed policy framing as an interactive cascading network activation. Cascading reflected the interactive process whereby information flows from the top through the middle to the bottom with limited interplay up the "waterfall." According to Entman, all actors in the cascade model behave as "cognitive misers" who seek to "satisfy" rather than articulate fully the details of a given issue. For issues that are congruent with existing perceptions (at all levels), he argues that the process of framing is readily achieved and accepted. Entman argues too that when issues do not fit preexisting notions, generating a smooth process of information dissemination becomes more difficult. Hence he proposes the media as an important instrument for public framing.

In this agenda framing model the public does have a role to play to direct information up the hierarchy, except that the media is seen to act as a go-between for citizen framing.

McGuire (1969) seems to support this approach when he develops what is called the converse model, which explains citizen preferences as non-monotonic due to variations in the probability of reception and acceptance. McGuire argues that citizens are moderately aware (receptive) and moderately partisan (acceptant) to change. He feels citizens are more malleable for typical events, and that the less aware are more malleable for high-intensity messages. In this discussion therefore the inclusion of the intensity of the message is seen to move the discussion toward advising the policy analyst that not all policy issues should be treated as equal and also that even different stages in the same issue could receive different levels of attention. (J. Zaller 1993).

2.1.2 Communication Theory

Critics of the view that policy is an elite realm, as presented to the positivist and elitist arguments, derive from communication theory. Communication theory discusses the influence that the media brings to bear on policy agendas, in particular the process by, which agendas are constructed or influenced. Thomas Birkland (2004) defines an agenda as a collection of the elements of public problems to, which at least some of the public and governmental officials are actively attentive. Agendas to Birkland range from concrete policy proposals to beliefs and exist at all levels of government and society (Birkland, 2004). In the communication theory, agenda setting is therefore the process whereby actors attempt to get issues on or keep issues off the agenda or otherwise attempt to control the content of the agenda.

The role of the media in setting the agenda is best described as a process "through, which the media day-by-day select and display the news. The process where editors and news directors focus attention and influence perceptions of what were the most important (salient) news events of the day." The media is seen to influence the salience of an issue and the significance people usually attach to issues. As evidence of the important role of the media in the agenda-setting function, McComby (2004) urges caution about the use of the media for policy agendas. He discusses a number of instances in, which the media created a sensation of fear over issues that were actually improving rather than worsening (McComby 2004).

2.1.3 Issue-Attention Theory

A strong critique of the populist approaches comes from Downs (1972). He provides a model that explains the level of attention given to an issue. He shows the salience of events to drive the public reaction rather than relying only on elites or the media (as the framing and agenda-setting models argued). Instead of viewing the media as the agenda-setting force, Downs argues that events drive public interest and that interest determines media coverage.

Downs presents a five-stage scheme of the issue-attention cycle, namely pre-problem, alarmed discovery and euphoric enthusiasm, realizing the cost, gradual decline of intense public interest, and post-problem. He argues that public attention rarely remains sharply focused upon any one issue for very long, even if such an issue is of critical importance to their country. He argues that the issue-attention cycle is more useful in presenting how societies react to agendas and how they are transformed in people's minds.

Downs says that the public perception of crises in life does not reflect changes in real conditions as much as it reflects the operation of a systematic cycle of heightening public interest and then increasing boredom with such issues. Hence for Downs, the issue-attention cycle is rooted both in the nature of a problem and in the way major communication media interact with the public. The cycle itself may vary in duration depending upon the particular issue involved.

2.1.3.1 Downs's Issue Attention Stages

Stage 1

2.1.3.1.1 The Pre-Problem Stage

The pre-problem stage, Downs (1972) argues, "prevails when some highly undesirable social condition exists but has not yet captured much public attention, even though some experts or interest group may have already been alarmed by it.

Stage 2

2.1.3.1.2 Alarmed Discovery and Euphoric Enthusiasm

Movement into the second stage occurs abruptly. As a result of some dramatic series of events that take place in the country, the public suddenly becomes both aware of and alarmed about the evils of a particular problem. For example, students clash with the police, and several are left dead. Or for some reason, the public or a segment of it become both aware of and alarmed about the evils of having a president who does things like a dictator, citing the excuse that he/she was popularly elected.

The alarmed discovery stage, Downs says, will be accompanied by euphoric enthusiasm about the country's ability to solve these problems or do something effective within a relatively short time. This combination of alarm and confidence results in part from the strong public pressure for political leaders to claim that every problem can be solved. The implication of such an expectation leads to thinking that every social problem can be eliminated and "every problem can be solved" syndrome.

Stage 3

2.1.3.1.3 Realizing the Cost

At this stage, there is a gradual and widespread realization by the public that the cost of solving the problem is very high. Some actors in the public realize that solving the problem would not only take a great deal of public resources but would also lead to a lot of sacrifices by quite a number of people or groups. Hence the public or groups start to realize that the cost of solving surpasses the benefits.

Stage 4

2.1.3.1.4 Gradual Decline of Intense Public Interest

As costs are perceived to be high, a gradual decline in the intensity of public interest in the problem starts. As more and more people realize how difficult and how costly to themselves a solution to the problem would be, several things happen. Some people just get discouraged by thinking about the problem. So they shelve or ignore such thoughts. Other people become bored by the issue, or most people just experience some combination of the last two feelings.

Consequently, the public desire to keep attention focused on the issues goes down or disappears completely. Downs argues that by this moment other issues are entering the 2 of the issue-attention circle.

Stage 5

2.1.3.1.5 The post-problem stage

In the final stage, an issue that has dominated public concern now moves into a prolonged limbo. It becomes a twilight realm of either lesser attention or a spasmodic recurrence of interest. At this stage, Downs argues, the issue has a different relation to the public attention than that, which prevailed in the pre-problem stage.

Figure 3: The stages of Downs's Issue-Attention Cycle Model

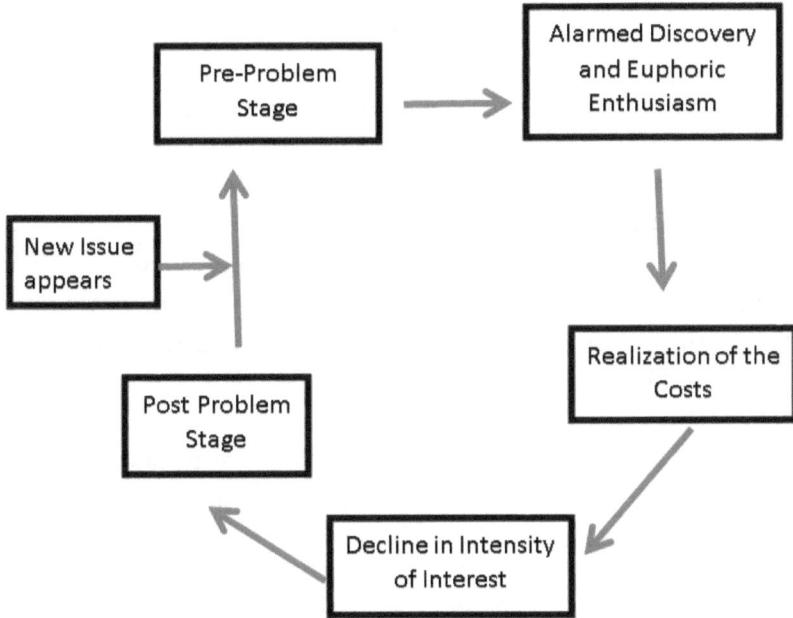

The Downs model has also been recently modified to show that at each stage a cycle can possibly develop within the cycle. A modified issue-attention cycle can show that issues can reignite the debate at several stages in the cycle. The diagram below shows that an issue can resurface at any point.

Figure 4: Modified Issue-Attention Cycle

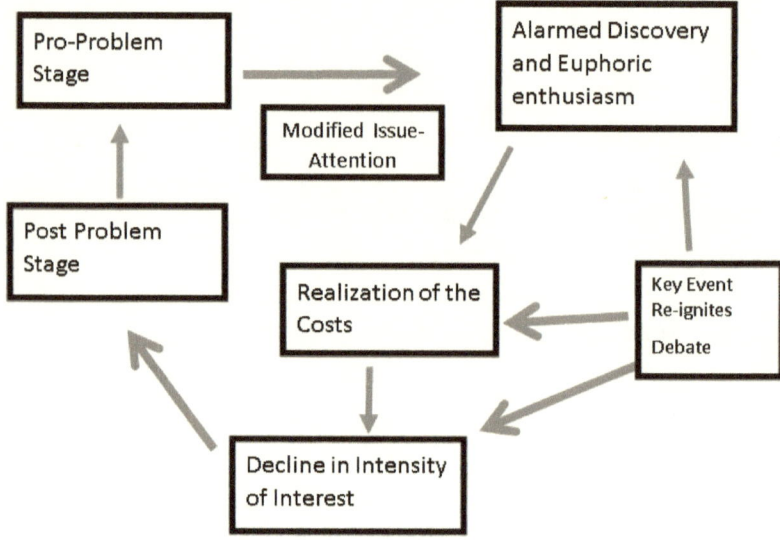

2.1.3.2 Which Problems Are Likely to Go Through the Cycle?

As in the approaches presented earlier, not all issues go through the "issue-attention cycle." They must possess to some degree three specific characteristics. First, the majority of persons in society are not suffering from the problem nearly as much as some minority (a numerical minority, not necessarily an ethnic one). Most people must not suffer directly enough from such problems to keep their attention riveted on them.

Second, the sufferings caused by the problem are generated by social arrangements that provide significant benefits to a majority or a powerful minority of the population.

Third, the problem must have no intrinsically exciting qualities—or must no longer have them. But when they have passed (or at least the media have stopped reporting them so intensively), public interest in the problems related to them declines sharply.

When all three of the above conditions exist concerning a given problem that has somehow captured public attention, the odds are great that it will soon move through the entire "issue-attention cycle" and therefore will gradually fade from the center of the stage. The first condition means that most people will not be continually reminded of the problem by their own suffering from it. The second condition means that solving the problem will require sustained attention and effort, plus fundamental changes in social institutions or behavior. This in turn means that significant attempts to solve it will be threatening to important groups in society. The third condition means that the media's sustained focus on this problem soon bores a majority of the public. As soon as the media realize that their emphasis on this problem is threatening many people and boring even more, they will shift their focus to some "new" problem.

Thus, as Marshall McLuhan has pointed out, it is largely the audience itself—the public—that "manages the news" by maintaining or losing interest in a given subject. As long as this pattern persists, we will continue to be confronted by a stream of "crises" involving particular social problems. Each will rise into public view, capture center stage for a while, and then gradually fade away as it is replaced by more fashionable issues moving into their "crisis" phases.

2.2 The Attention Span Approach

Other observers of policy agendas see the challenge of agenda setting not so much about the declining interest an issue may capture but rather the attention span.

The attention span is regarded as the amount of time that a person can concentrate on a task without becoming distracted. It is argued that the ability to focus one's attention on a task is crucial for the achievement of one's goals. Hence, to understand how issues get within the policy process, one needs to understand the attention span for society and not only government officials.

For policy analysis, two types of human attention have been identified, namely focused attention and sustainable attention.

2.2.1 Focused Attention

- Focused attention is regarded as a short-term response to a stimulus that has drawn attention. The attention span for this level has been found to be very brief, with a maximum span, without any lapse at all that could be as short as 8 seconds. This level of attention, it is argued, was attracted by, say, a ringing of the telephone or other unexpected occurrences. After a few seconds, it is likely that the person will look away, return to previous tasks, or think about something else.

2.2.2 Sustainable Attention

- Sustained attention involves the level of attention that produces consistent results on a task over time. If the task involves handling fragile objects, such as hand-washing delicate crystal glasses, then a person showing sustained attention stays on task and does not break any dishes. A person who loses focus does break a glass or stops washing the dishes to do something else. This approach seems to suggest that people are generally capable of a longer attention span when they are doing something that they find enjoyable or intrinsically motivating.

Attention is also noted to increase if the person is able to perform the task fluently, compared to a person who has difficulty performing the task or who is just learning the task. Fatigue, hunger, noise, and emotional stress are also noted to reduce attention span. Further, findings suggest that after a person's attention has shifted from a topic or task, he/she may restore it by taking a rest, doing a different kind of activity, changing mental focus, or deliberately choosing to refocus on the previous subject.

Similarly, people with a longer attention span are better able to remain absorbed in a particular activity without distraction. Those with a short attention span are seen to be easily distracted. On policy issues they tend to shift positions too quickly. They are also seen to be fickle at policy positions. Their short attention span leads them to take positions that require answers now or else positions are changed or forgotten. At times because of short attention span the policy analyst may face last-minute breakdown in policy debates as positions change.

2.3 The Driving Force – Pressure – Approach,

Some see policy analysis as an organized way in, which society reacts to problematic issues. It is argued that policy analysts first face societal driving forces. The forces create pressure on society. The pressures lead to an unacceptable state of affairs. The unacceptable state leads to impact on society, which in turn leads to response to solve the problem.

Figure 5: The Driving Force-Pressure-State-Impact Response Approach

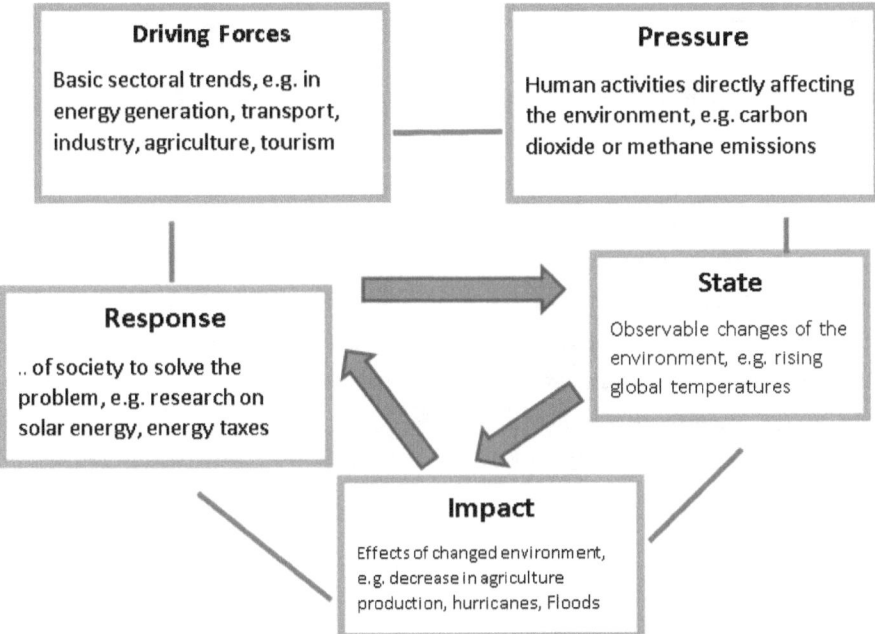

2.4 The Policy Analyst and Policy Agendas

From these worldviews where agendas come from we note one common view: that policy agendas are a list of subjects or problems to, which the government, individuals, or organizations are paying attention. The stakeholders expect that government may do something about the issues in question.

The challenge in policy design therefore, is for the policy analyst to put attention to "what is on the table?" "What are the content of these policy agendas?" "What factors are driving the policy issues?"

2.4.1 Designing Policy Issues from Agendas

The policy agendas are many, and they originate from inside and outside the organization. However, policy agendas need to move into policy issues. The policy analyst should at times "speak truth to power" by making policy issues visible; the policy analyst must also maintain the momentum so as to transform policy issues into political or administrative action.

The policy analyst faces the challenge of getting a policy issue as an "idea whose time has come." This process is tricky. The policy analyst has to move a policy agenda into policy issues and then into the short list of policy issues receiving attention. So other than seeing policy analysis as purely an objective presentation, the policy analyst must also know how to advocate and persuade the decision process to see that the selected policy issues are attended to rather than others. The analyst's work involves vying for issue attention. It involves "determining where an issue is positioned in the policy agenda queue, how law makers, ministers and other influential stakeholders are thinking and talking about it. It also involves speaking for those not on the table and the powerless" (Blent 2007).

CHAPTER 3

Managing the Policy Process

Two models are popular and used by policy analysts to contribute to the policy process. In this section, we show how a policy analyst can work with the rational and policy process cycles model in the policy process.

3.1 The Linear Model

Variously called the linear or rational approach to policy analysis, this model is perhaps the most widely held view of the way a policy is made. The linear model outlines policy making as a problem solving process that is rational, balanced, objective, and analytical. In this model the policy analyst makes decisions in a series of sequential phases. She/he starts with the identification of a problem or issue and ends with a set of activities to solve or deal with the problem. Policy analysis is "speaking truth to power" by using analytical skill. (Windasky 1984).

Figure 6: The Linear Model

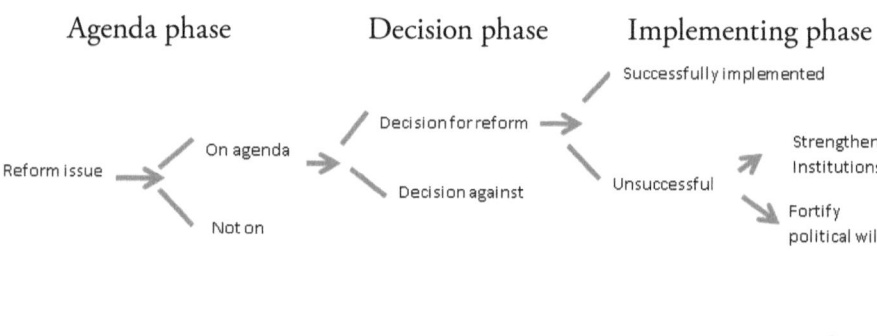

Source: Grindle and Thomas (1990)

In the linear model the analyst assumes that participants would approach the issues rationally, going through logical stages and carefully considering all relevant information. If policies do not achieve what they were intended to achieve, then blame is often not laid on the policy itself but rather on political or managerial failure in implementation (Juma and Clark 1995).

3.2 Working with the Rational Approach

The policy analyst must know and understand the key stages in the policy process and then in each stage use relevant tools to make the analysis. Also at each stage key questions are posed, and the answers help in problem solving. The challenge is to come up with policy-relevant information at each stage of the analysis. Below are the key stages and what the policy analyst does in each stage.

Stage 1

3.2.1 Design Policy Problem

The first stage is to define the problem at hand. This is done by asking the following questions:

- What is the problem that requires solving?

- How do we know it exists?

At this stage the policy analyst must guide against several pitfalls; e.g.:

i) looking for simple and obvious problems;

ii) taking problematic situations as problems;

iii) accepting powerful stakeholders' definition of problems; and

iv) thinking that all problems can be solved by using policies.

The policy analyst must state the problem meaningfully by

i) continually redefining the problem in the light of what is possible and trying to eliminate irrelevant issues;

ii) determining the magnitude and extent of the problem;

iii) eliminating ambiguity in the problem statement;

iv) always questioning the accepted thinking about the problem;

v) questioning the traditional standards and formulation of the problem;

vi) clarifying the problem by specifying objectives to be achieved if the problem is solved;

vii) thinking about who is concerned about the problem and why; and

viii) questioning the authority and power of interested parties.

3.2.1.1 Clarifying Objectives

It should be noted that every time a policy problem is identified, it is good to clarify it by adopting some statement of goals and objectives. The goals are what the adopted policy will accomplish.

Goals are broad formal and long-term problem solving achievements that are desired. Goals are translated into policy objectives. Policy objectives are more concrete statements about desired and end states. They often have timetables and targets.

3.2.1.2 Objective Criteria

The policy analyst must come up with criteria by, which to compare how close different proposed policy alternatives will come to meeting the goals of solving the problem. A well designed criterion will be a set of rules to follow in analyzing and comparing different policy alternatives.

The criteria and their measures should be unambiguous and straightforward. The application of these criteria should produce uniform results no matter who uses them. Hence care must be taken when specifying the criteria and measures, since most problem statements have fuzzy or conflicting goals.

From the field of practice there are at the minimum six criteria that are always used. We shall illustrate how they are used in another chapter. But it is important to mention the following commonly used criteria:

1. economic criteria, which might involve several such criteria

2. equity criteria, which measure how benefits and costs are distributed

3. political criteria, including political acceptability and appropriateness, legality, responsiveness, and so on

4. administrative criteria, which require considerations of commitment, competency, capacity, support, and so on

5. technical criteria, which include assessing technical feasibility and effectiveness

6. social criteria, including societal support or rejection, culture, and traditional criteria

It is always important to be innovative when coming up with the criteria that is relevant to the policy problem at hand.

Stage 2

3.2.2 Designing Policy Options

After the problem has been defined, the next step involves identifying possible solutions to the problem, usually called policy alternatives. At this stage the policy analyst must generate several alternatives, which are later reduced to a manageable number. The practice has been to reduce policy alternatives to between four and five. We usually start with status quo as the first alternative. It is an option which assumes continuing with what has been happening. Then one generates an option radically different from the status quo. In between are many options. One can add as many options as humanly possible. At this stage it is useful to brainstorm many alternatives.

3.2.2.1 Typical Sources of Policy Alternatives

There are common sources of policy alternatives used in the analysis. They include

i) the status quo;

ii) redefining the problem from others' point of view, including opponents of any change;

iii) applying political, economic, and other constraint analysis to the idea;

iv) doing a quick survey of literature, case studies; and

v) using analogies, peer review, or common opinion.

3.2.2.2 Pitfalls

Policy analysts encounter several pitfalls at this stage. One needs to avoid the common pitfalls, which include the following:

i) quickly closing the process of problem definition and searching for solutions to address wrongly defined problems

ii) taking policy option preferences too soon in the search for alternatives, therefore ruling out too quickly other alternative options

iii) trying to criticize new ideas generated by others or actually failing to listen for other alternatives

iv) tending to stick to old ways and discard alternatives

Stage 3

3.2.3 Comparing Alternatives

In stage 2 options are identified. In stage 3 the process taken is to choose the alternative that will best resolve the policy problem.

The challenge in this stage is how one chooses the methods and techniques and how to apply them correctly. However, the process is a simple one. One needs to do the following:

i) Choose a format to present the identified alternatives.

ii) Carry out the following actions on each identified alternative:

   a) Identify the strengths and weaknesses of each alternative.

   b) Describe the worst and best case scenario for each identified option.

   c) Do an in-depth analysis of those alternatives, which made the first cut on the above criteria.

iii) Estimate the expected outcomes and possible impact of those that got through the initial test and examine, which alternative has predicted outcomes and impact that meet the stated goals.

iv) Rank order the outcomes of each alternative and where possible weigh each criteria accordingly. (See chapter 10 for technique to weight options.)

At the end of this stage you should be able to rank order alternatives and pick the alternative that best meets your policy goals. At times one may confront the apparent trade-offs. The best approach is to have an evidence-based comparison.

3.3 The Process Approach

The policy process involves a specified process through which the policy analyst participates in the policy process. There are a number of activities, some purely for policymakers and others for policy analysts. Therefore, the policy analyst should create a niche in this process. The policy analytical processes are used to organize the analyst's contribution in the policy process. The commonly used process in this regard is the policy cycle framework.

3.3.1 The Policy Cycle

Policy cycles have been used to organize and to describe policy processes. In policy cycles, we conceive the policy process as a sequence of steps from issue identification through to implementation and evaluation. Therefore, a policy cycle is a tool that a policy analyst can use for analyzing the development of a policy item. It can also be referred to as a "stage approach." However, it emphasizes the link between policy design, implementation, monitoring, and evaluation.

The policy cycle approaches redefine the role of a policy analyst as not only embracing policy design but also involving follow-through on implementation, to monitor and evaluate the success of the adopted policy.

There exist several policy cycle approaches used in policy analysis. They run from few to multiple stages:

3.3.2 The Multiple Stages Approach

What is common in policy cycle approaches is the most widely held view of the way policy is made. It outlines policy-making as a problem solving process, which is rational, balanced, objective, and analytical. In the model, decisions are made in a series of sequential phases, starting with the identification of a problem or issue and ending with a set of activities. Then outcomes are assessed to determine whether the initially selected alternative did resolve the initial problem.

The model comprises several steps, from four to as many as nine. However, the common logic of the policy cycle models is moving from first step to last step. The phases commonly presented are the following:

Step 1

- Recognizing and defining the nature of the issue to be dealt with

Step 2

- Identifying possible courses of action to deal with the issue

Step 3

- Weighing up the advantages and disadvantages of each of these alternatives

Step 4

- Choosing the option that offers the best solution

Step 5

- Monitoring the Implementation of the policy

Step 6

- Evaluating the policy outcomes

The policy process is presented as a road map starting from issue identification all the way to implementation. At each stage the policy analyst uses specific techniques to improve decision making or to shape informed advice to policymakers. It is evident that the policy cycle approaches emphasize problem solving as the major aim of policy analysis. Figure 7 is an illustration of commonly used policy cycles.

From Figure 7 we note that the policy cycle approaches are really an improvement on the rational approach. While the rational approach activities end up with a recommendation, the policy cycle adds two more stages in the policy process, monitoring (stage 5) and evaluating (stage 6) the policy outcomes.

Figure 7: Policy Cycle and Policy-Relevant Information

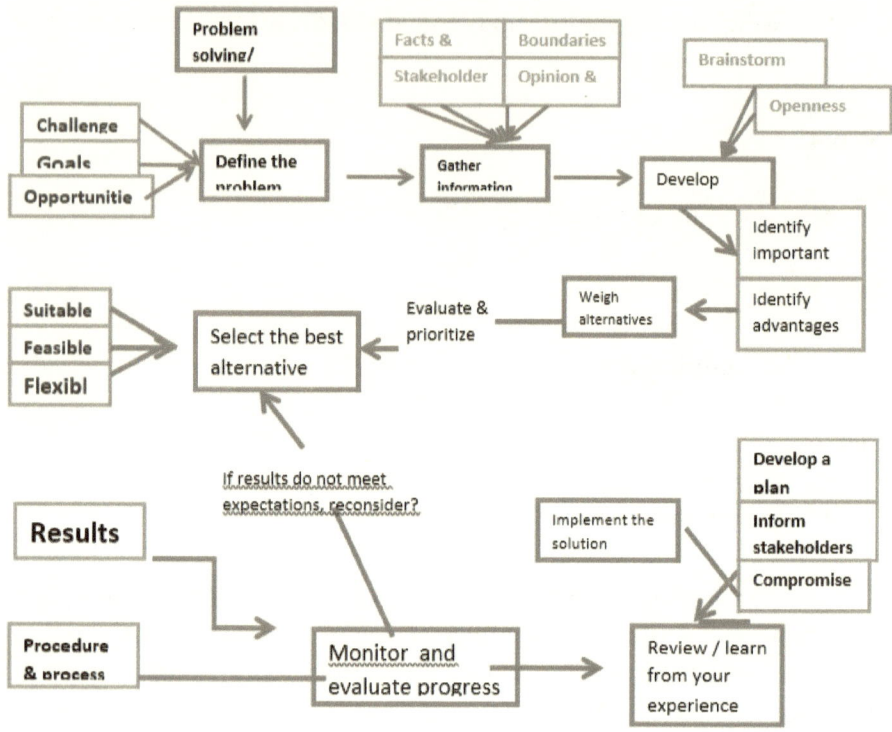

Figures 8 and 9 present some of the commonly used illustrations of the policy process. Figure 8 shows how the process has been used in a public service context. It introduces the role of the citizen, the cabinet, and the Public Service.

Figure 8: The New Policy Life Cycle

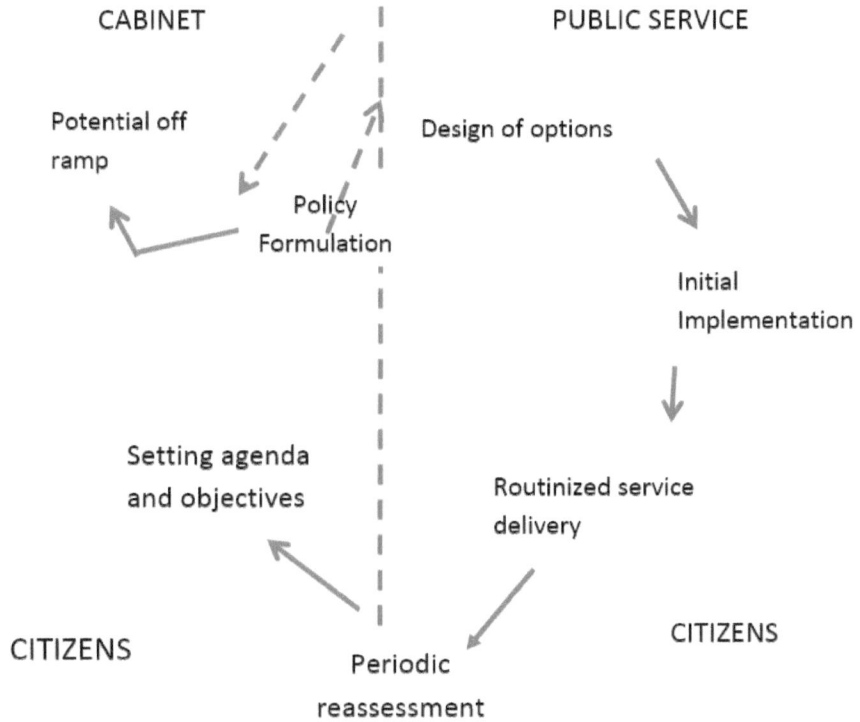

Source:

Figure 9 is an elaboration of how <u>Australia</u> has worked with the policy process model.

Figure 9: An Australian Policy Cycle Model

Source: Bridgman and Davis 2004

What is common to Figures 7, 8, and 9 are the analytical processes, which are summarized in Figure 10.

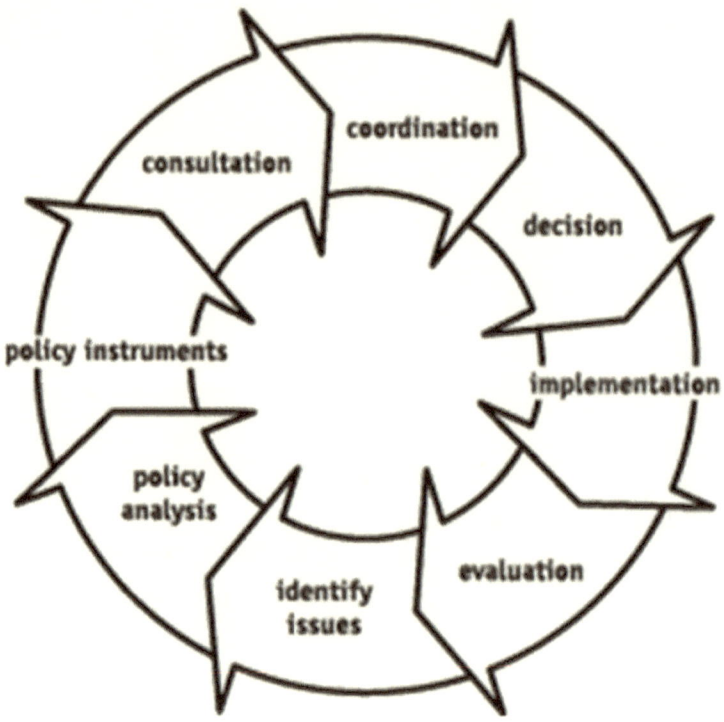

Figure 10: Analytical Process

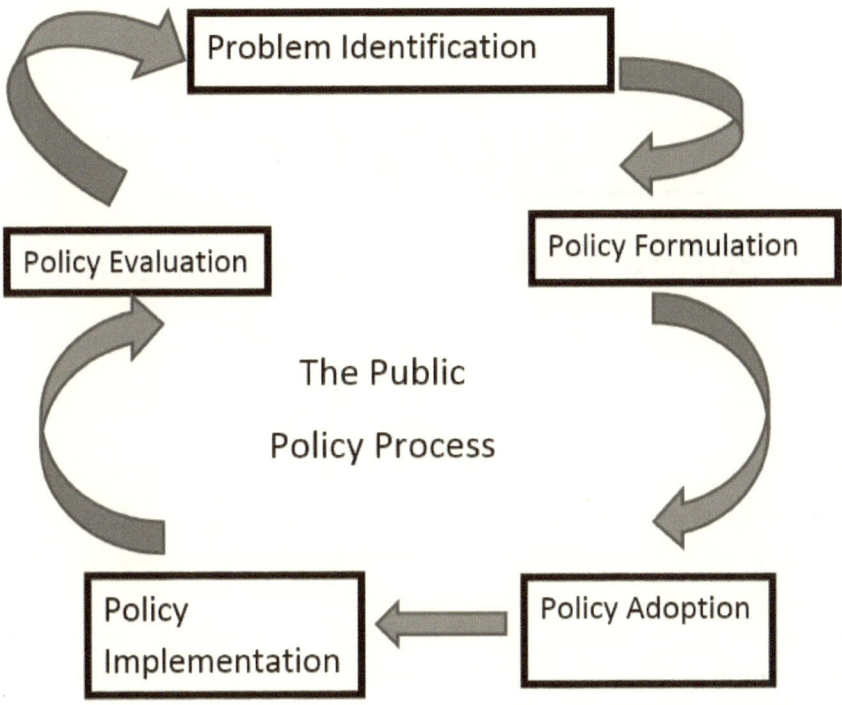

In this chapter we note that policy analysis is determining, which of various alternative policies will best achieve a given set of goals in light of the relations between the policies and the goal. However, policy analysis can be divided into two major fields: descriptive and prescriptive. Analysis of policy is analytical and descriptive if it attempts to explain policies and their development. Analysis for policy is prescriptive if it is involved with formulating policies and proposals (e.g., to improve social welfare). The area of interest and the purpose of analysis determine what type of analysis is conducted.

CHAPTER 4

Policy Problem Identification and Structuring

Policies are used as instruments for problem solving. Therefore, designing a policy involves knowing what is desired. Hence it is important for the policy analyst to be very clear about what is and what is desired. "A problem expresses the difference between the hoped for and the actual situation." It is only after structuring a problem that we can come up with a policy intervention. Thus any and every experienced policy analyst will advise that the most difficult stage in the policy process is coming up with a well-defined policy problem. It is often noted that structuring a policy problem is not an easy exercise. The approach therefore is for the policy analyst to be systematic in understanding the real problem from its manifestations. Two important questions must be addressed, namely:

a) Does a policy problem exist?

b) Can anything be done about it?

If the answers are no, then there is no point in going forward.

The reason for asking the above two questions is to avoid the common pitfalls generally encountered in policy analysis:

1. accepting the manifestation of the problem as a problem

2. looking only for the simple and obvious signs

3. thinking that any and all problems need a policy solution

4. confusing the need for short- versus long-term solutions

5. confusing the values of individuals versus those of the organization or collectivities

The challenge at this stage of the policy process and analysis is to state the problem meaningfully and clearly. This is usually done by carrying out some preliminary assessment of the problem. This would include the following:

a) determining the magnitude and extent of the problem

b) continually redefining the problem in the light of what is possible

c) eliminating irrelevant material

d) questioning the accepted thinking about the problem

e) questioning initial formulations of the problem

f) backing the arguments with data

g) locating similar policy analyses done elsewhere

h) making sense out of ambiguity

i) clarifying policy objectives

j) resolving conflicting goals

k) focusing on the central, critical factors

l) identifying who is concerned, and why

    m) discerning what power concerned parties have

    n) making a quick estimate of resources required to deal with the problem[2]

4.1 Problem Identification Considerations

Traditional and common practice is to think that policy analysis is an orderly and often a linear process. Traditional thinking puts it that "policy analysis is a technical process of working from a problem and the challenge is to get the right solution to relate to that policy problem." But best practice in policy analysis shows that "policy analysis fails most often because we formulate the wrong problem than because we choose the wrong solution" (Dunn 1988). So the policy analyst should not neglect the importance of policy problem structuring.

4.2 Policy Problems

Policy problems can be classified as "well, moderately or ill structured" (Dunn 1984). Well-structured problems are easily solved by administrative procedure, rules, and regulations while moderately structured problems need only strategic thinking. But ill-structured problems beat all current knowledge and any means of understanding them. They are indeed wicked problems (Rittel 1973).

Wicked policy problems have properties of social complexity. Social complexity is seen in the number of and diversity of stakeholders. In policy issues many stakeholders are involved. The more stakeholders are involved, the more socially complex the policy problem. Hence "solutions to wicked problems are not right or wrong, they are simply better, worse, good enough or not good enough" (Rittel 1973). Solutions to wicked problems are not true-or-false but rather good-or-bad.

Wicked problems are very complex, and the policy analyst has to be creative and innovative just to understand them. Horst Rittel says that the

---

[2]   http://web.csulb.edu/~msaintg/ppa670/670steps.htm

policy analyst cannot understand a problem until he/she has "developed" a solution. However, every solution that the policy analyst gives leads to new aspects of the problem, which will require further adjustment of the potential solutions (Rittel 1973). "One cannot understand the problem without knowing about the context." It is indeed a matter of creativity to design potential solutions, and often it will require professional judgment to come up with a problem statement that is valid, persuasive, and can be resolve.

It is important to appreciate that there is no "definitive problem"; the analyst also faces a situation where there is no "definitive solution." At times the determination of a solution will not be to come up with some objective formula or model. Problem statements and proposed solutions will be analyzed in a social context depending on the stakeholders' independent values and goals. It is understandable therefore why a "good policy" under liberals/Democrats will be seen to be useless under conservatives/Republicans! Mixed presentations of the same phenomena often arise as different stakeholders always think they are certain that their way of seeing the world and/or the problem is the correct one.

4.3 Policy Problem Conceptualization

The policy analyst must first aim at knowing and understanding how policy issues are identified, conceptualized, and defined by different stakeholders (Vesely 2007). He/she also needs to know why some societal conditions become defined as policy problems and others do not. Also what are the reasons and consequences of different designing or framing of policies?

Problem structuring must therefore aim at providing a good and precise formulation and designing of policy problems so that the problem can be resolved.

4.4 Techniques for Problem Structuring

Several techniques are presented here that can be used in structuring a policy problem.

4.4.1 Problem Sensing

After the problematic situation has been transformed into a problem, one must make sure that the boundaries of the problem are clear to avoid trying to think one can solve all issues in one intervention. The analyst needs to be able to describe the formal problem in detail.

4.4.1.1 Illustration

A city council has been experiencing an increase in road fatalities. A number of young drivers have met their deaths through these road accidents. Data show that road fatalities have become a major public complaint as these fatalities have become publically unacceptable.

4.4.2 Describing the Problem

To design a policy, we need to describe the problem it is supposed to resolve. This requires unpacking the problematic situation.

To make a problem, we have to ask some key questions on the problematic situation. We have to get more detailed data and information on some key questions:

1. What?

2. Where?

3. When?

4. Who?

5. How?

6. Why?

There are different ways this problematic situation can be structured as a policy problem. For instance, we can formulate several problem issues as follows:

Increase in road fatalities started with an increase in unlicensed drivers.

Or

Increase in road fatalities seems to be related to increase in volume of traffic and no expansion in road infrastructure.

Or

Increase in road fatalities seems to be related to increase in underage drivers.

When we use the problem description technique, it can help us clarify the problem. From these initial descriptions of the problem, we can use evidence-based analysis to describe the policy problem accurately.

4.5 Problem Clarification Tool

What?

We need to answer some key questions on the problematic situation, which will help us design the nature of the problems. "The question 'What is going on?' creates anguished answers and leads to sensing, while the question 'What?' leads to describing what is happening or not happening. At this stage the approach is to try to name the problematic situation. Giving the problem a name is important. The way you name it will influence the way you design the policy and later how you design measurement of success. The policy problem should also be seen as a situation that occurs between what "should be" and "what is."

This stage includes gap analysis. The gap is between what we would want to see and what we are seeing now. It can also be what is between some standard and our current performance, set goals, or vision or what we are expected to do from some global standard.

Figure 11 below illustrates the use of mind mapping tools to structure the "What?" question. It shows that the mind can generate a lot of answers to the "What is going on?" question.

Figure 11: Using Mind Mapping Tools to Clarify the Policy Problem

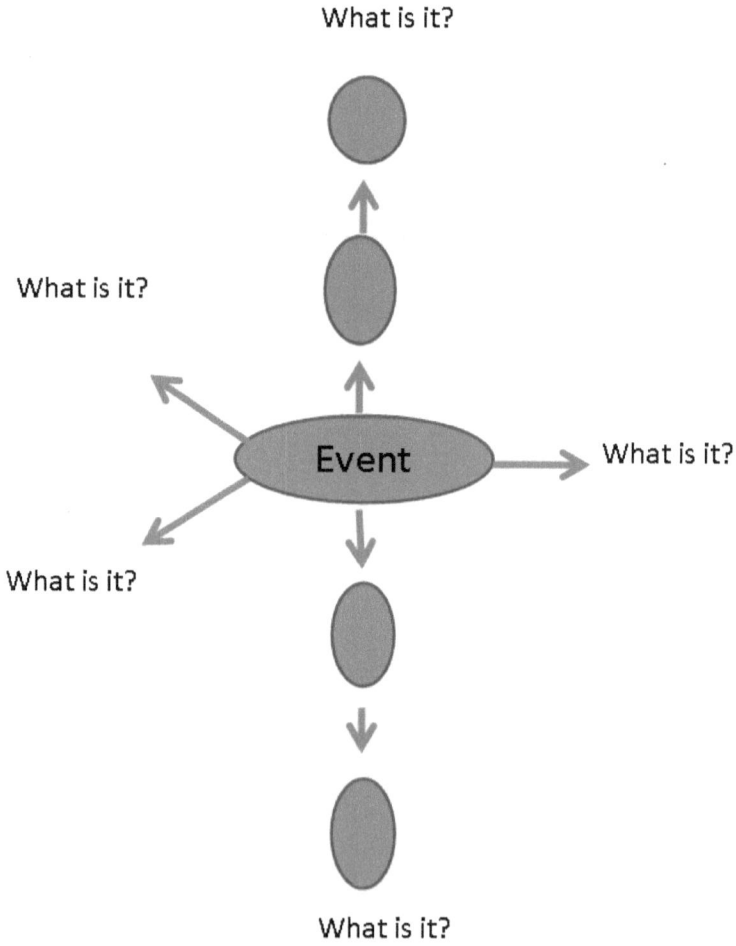

The event may be noted as the problematic situation. "What is it?" mind mapping helps us to move from the "problematic" to "naming." The answer to "What is it?" names and narrows our understanding of the problem.

When?

"When does it generally occur?" helps us perceive issues not as discrete events but as a course of action, which if not handled within a period/ that time will lead to "system" collapse or irrelevance (Mwape 2002). Answers to these questions require evidence-based presentations. It can also involve discovering the frequency of the events that lead to the problematic situation, or it could simply aim to understand the timing of the events taken to be problematic.

Where?

This question puts the problem into its "space." The levels of problem space can be analyzed as

a)   global space;

b)   national space;

c)   sector space;

d)   organization space; and

e)   individual space.

The issue is to understand where the problem occurs. In most policy problems the location will be a useful tool that limits the scope and nature of the policy intervention.

Who?

Who is being or will be affected by the problem if not resolved? We want to know who is affected negatively or positively. Who has the power of influence over the problem definition, adoption, and/or implementation? Who has interest on the issue? Who has no interest in the issue?

The "who" question can be answered using stakeholder analysis.

Placing stakeholders like this will help a policy analyst to create a proper advocacy system.

4.5.1 Problem-Structuring Exercise

Illustration: Unemployment among university graduates

Country A has been receiving complaints about the increased number of unemployed among university graduates (i.e., those unable to find jobs) and those becoming unemployed. The number of unemployed is becoming alarming every year and has become unacceptable.

Exercise: Using the problem clarification tool, describe the problem.

Problem-Structuring Exercise

Illustration: Revenue Shortfalls

A municipal council is facing dwindling revenue. A contract cash flow analysis shows that the council will not implement the planned 80 percent of capital development. The shortfall is creating apprehension in the committee as service quality is also falling quickly. Sometimes there is no water supply for several days.

Exercise: Using the problem clarification tool, describe the problem being faced by the municipality.

Figure 12: Illustration

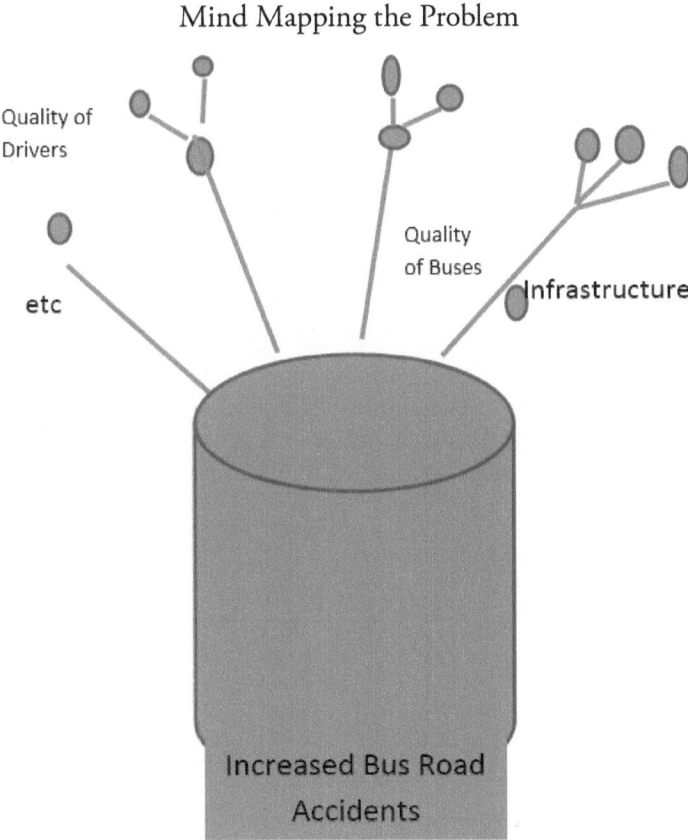

Mind Mapping the Problem

Quality of Drivers

Quality of Buses

Infrastructure

etc

Increased Bus Road Accidents

The problematic situation is the increased number of bus accidents in the country. A lot of people have been injured or have died. Mind mapping using "What is it?" helps us come down to problem specification. The illustration in Figure 12 above shows that the problems are varied. It could be quality of buses, quality of drivers, or poor infrastructure.

4.6 Ranking Policy Problems

Answering the "What is it?" question will result in a number of possible policy problem statements. However, not all possible policy problems will be plausible and actionable (Dunn 1984). Therefore, we need to filter some of the possible policy problems using the policy problem ranking tool. In ranking, we consider the following:

- frequency

- urgency

- importance

- feasibility

Frequency

The key question is examining the frequency of the problem. The question is whether it happens often or rarely.

Urgency

Refers to the urgency of the problem. Should it be solved now or can it wait?

Importance

It is analyzed from the point of view of the stakeholders. How do the stakeholders view the problem in their lives?

Feasibility

Is the problem probable or difficult? Can it be handled using public policy or other interventions?

How It Is Done

To do the ranking, we need a process that first identifies the problems through peer review or brainstorming. Then a table will be drawn as illustrated below:

Table 1: Ranking Policy Problems

Problem	Feasibility	Equity	Frequency	Urgency	Importance	Total
A						
B						
C						
D						
E						

4.6.1 Scoring

1. This exercise is best done in a group of four to five.

2. Each person in the group should give a score out of ten—one (1) taken to be the lowest and ten the highest score for each element.

3. The group comes to a consensus on the score based on evidence they have.

4. After the scoring, add scores for each element.

5. Total the row for each problem statement.

6. Standardize the scores by dividing the total for each problem by number of elements used (five in this case). The standardized totals help us prioritize the problem. The highest score will be taken to have the highest priority.

Table 2: Illustration Ranking of Policy Problems

	Criteria					
Problem	Feasibility	Equity	Frequency	Urgency	Importance	Total
A	2	7	5	6	5	25/5 = 5
B	7	5	7	7	8	3 4 / 5 = 6.8
C	9	4	5	2	6	2 6 / 5 = 5.2
D	4	8	7	5	7	3 1 / 5 = 6.2

From the ranking problem B is on average ranked to be a first priority problem, and A is a last priority problem.

4.6.2 Weighting Policy Problems

Policy problems don't manifest themselves at the same level of feasibility, frequency, importance, equity, etc. So most often the policy analyst must give weights or do the problem measurements to be able to rank-order the problems.

The table below shows an illustration of such weighting.

Table 3: Weighting Policy Problems

Problem	Feasibility	Equity	Frequency	Urgency	Important	Total
Weighting						
A	2.0	1.5	0.5	2.5	3.0	

B	SxW	SxW	SxW	SxW	SxW	
C	SxW	SxW	SxW	SxW	SxW	
D	SxW	SxW	SxW	SxW	SxW	
	SxW	SxW	SxW	SxW	SxW	

Note

S stands for scores on each element

W stands for weight given to each element

4.7 Cause and Effect Analysis

Once we have clarified the problem, we have moved from the problematic situation to the formal specification of the policy problem. When the latter is done, we should further analyze the factors causing this problem. Mind mapping and decision tree tools are best used to analyze the cause and effect of policy problems.

What is causing it?

Understanding the causes of the problem is an indirect way to infer the problem. After designing the problem, we cannot move to thinking about the solutions without understanding the factors that are causing it. This is because if we can identify the critical causes of the problem, we will be able to prioritize the causes and hopefully come up with an appropriate policy intervention.

4.7.1 Process of Analyzing Causes

We start with a problem statement; then we can use the mind mapping tool again to understand factors causing the problem. Here we take the "cause" as the key policy problem to be resolved. The thinking is that if we can identify the causes we are better placed to treat the problem.

Below is an illustration of how to use the mind mapping tool to understand the causes of the problem.

Figure 13: Cause Analysis Using Mind Mapping

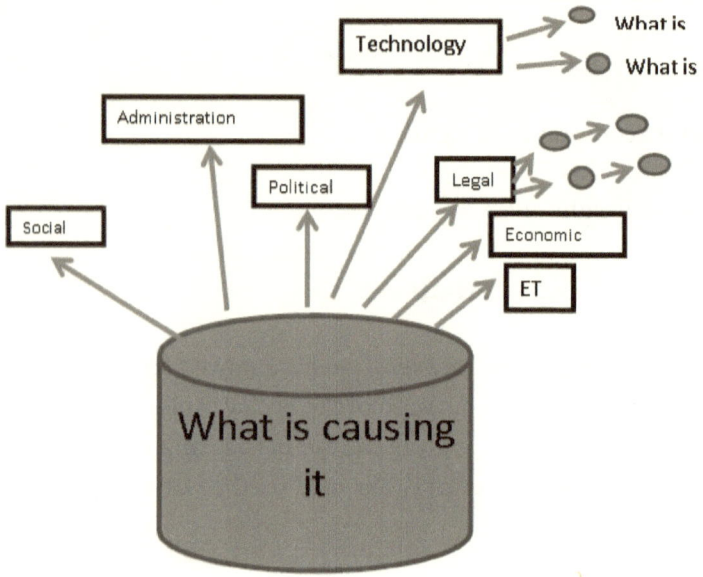

The figure shows macro factors that can likely cause a problem. We can break these macro factors, into meso factors all the way to micro factors. For example, if the problem is increased unemployment among graduates, one macro cause might be economic factors. We identify such economic factors, and for each economic factor we break it into meso factors, and for each meso factor we break out the micro factors. The figure below illustrates this logic of thinking and getting to "what is causing it."

In the figure we note that every issue is analyzed and related to the key problematic situation. Then each cause factor is operationalized to the level that is clear enough for policy action.

Figure 14: Cause of Unemployment among Graduates

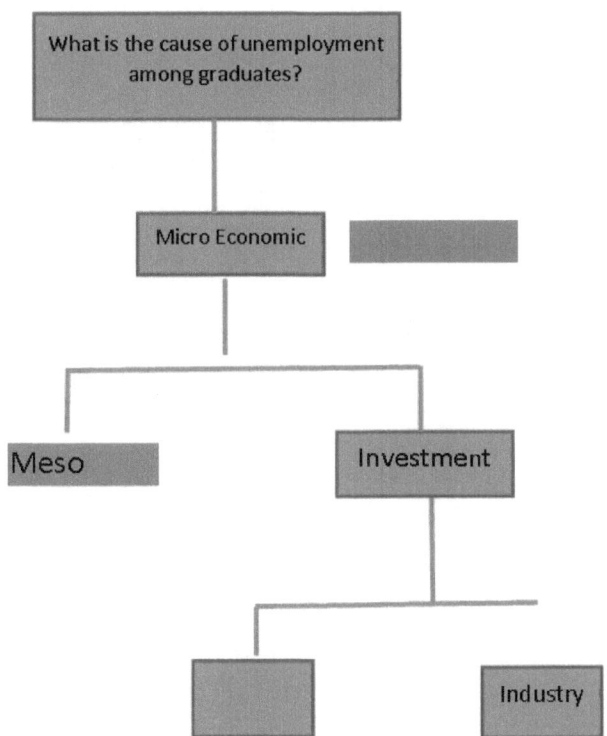

4.7.2 Problem Tree to Clarify the Cause and Effect

Another tool for understanding the problem as to its cause and effect is the so-called problem tree. This method allows the policy analyst to clarify the causes and the effects of the specified problem. With the problem tree tool, the policy analyst is able to understand:

a) The causes (roots) of a policy problem,
b) The core policy problem itself, and
c) The policy problem's effects.

Illustration of a Problem Tree

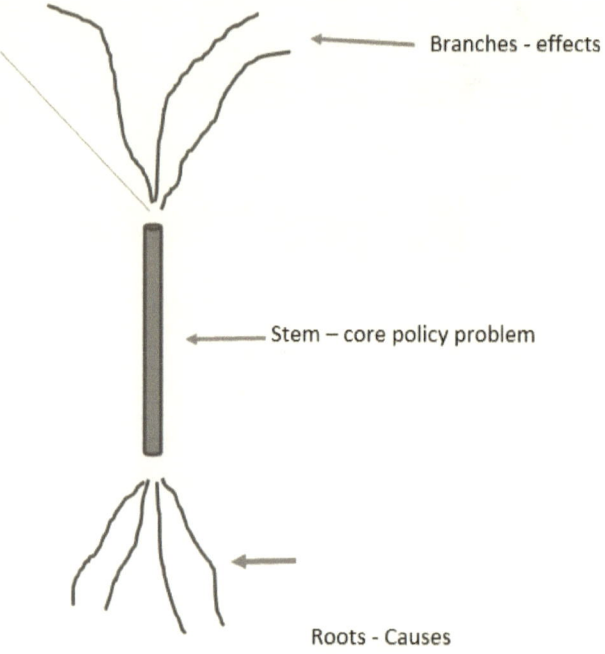

Branches - effects

Stem – core policy problem

Roots - Causes

Using the problem tree analysis, cause-effect understanding can turn out to be very interesting and complicated. If well done, several root-causes and effects of the problem can be generated. It also helps the analyst distinguish causes from problems and problems from effects.

It also enables the analyst to appreciate the wicked problem mess. With these methods we should be able to rank first-, second-, and third-level causes and similarly first-, second-, and third-level effects on a stated problem. Apart from level analysis, we can also see the interconnectedness in causes and effects.

Figure 15 shows these hierarchies of causes and effects.

Figure 15: Illustration of a Policy Problem Tree Tool

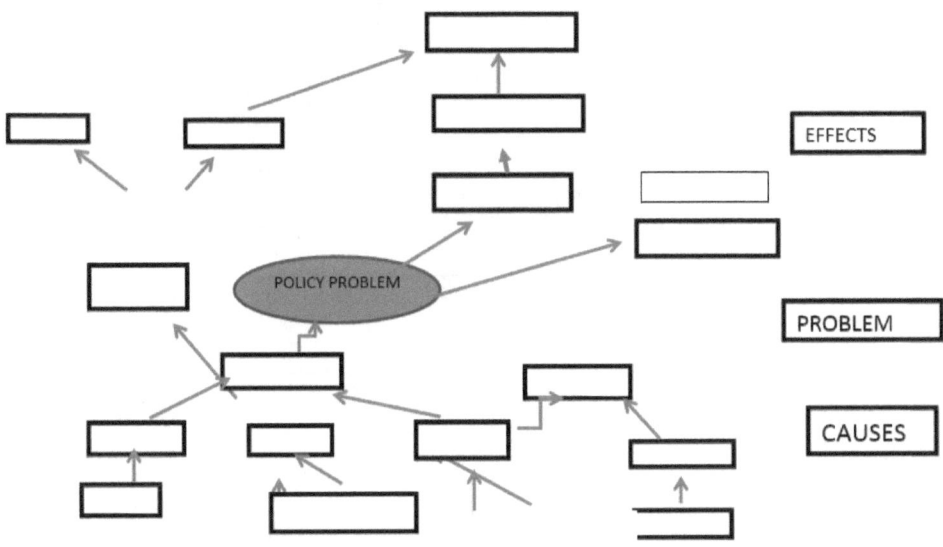

The third level tend to be broad cause-effects. They become narrow as we move up the levels. In Figure 11, we note that the causes of frequent accidents in "Nairobi town" are a variety of factors from infrastructure to technology to drivers. In each of these macro factors, we can design relevant micro causes. Group brainstorming the process can generate quite a good number of items as each participant moves out of the box. The best way to work with the problem tree tools is to move downward. First identify the major problem, then determine factors that underlie this major problem and then finally the causes of those factors (Wikibooks 2015).

At the end of the exercise, the policy analyst will get too many causes for the policy problem under discussion. We need to weight these definitions of causes to be able to see the immediate causes, secondary causes, and so on. The challenge for the analyst is to identify the direct causes of the policy problem. Similarly, when analyzing effects, we can put them in a hierarchy of effects. Several categorizations can be used to help have a clear appreciation of these effects. We can group effects as immediate, intermediate, or long-term. Hence using a problem tree can give us a number of separate or interrelated policy interventions to help resolve the policy problem.

Figure 16: Illustration of a Policy Problem Tree Tool

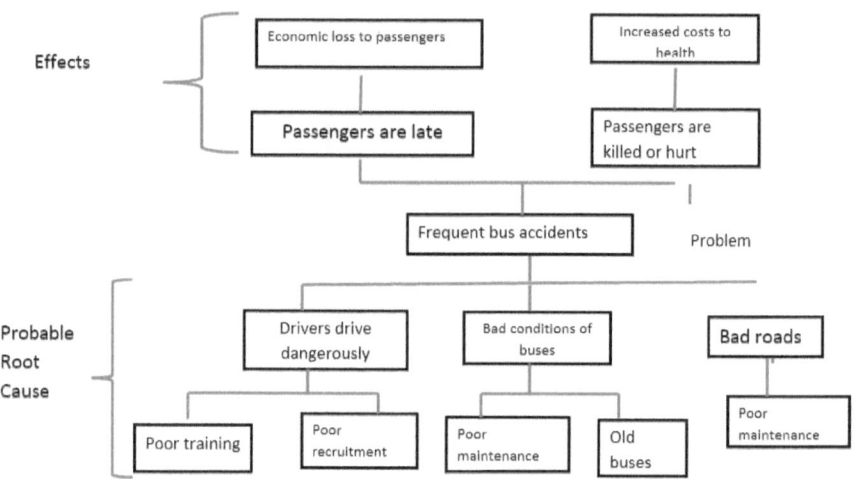

When using the problem tree tool, the brainstorming group should always use the evidence-based approach to describe the policy problem accurately. See some illustrations from my student group work below.

4.7.2.1 How to Work with a Problem Tree

During our MBA classes we have over time developed a system that simulates stakeholders. Students form groups that take positions as if they were policy stakeholders.

In this workshop students are able to create a balanced analysis while taking account of different and often conflicting ideas. The aim of this exercise is for students to link the identified problem together in a problem tree. The second challenge of the brainstorming is to develop the cause-effect relationship through a problem tree. The outcome of the brainstorming can be very complex. In Figures 17 to 20 below, the class generated many causes-effects of graduate unemployment in the country.

Figure 17: Cause-Effect Analysis of Graduate Employment

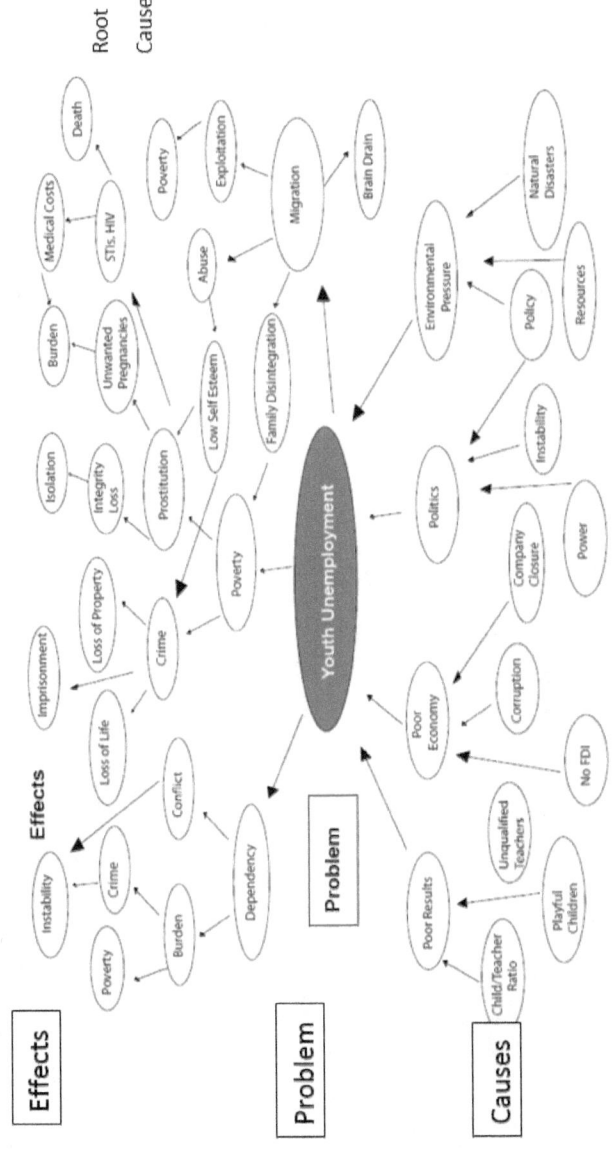

57

Figure 18: Youth Unemployment

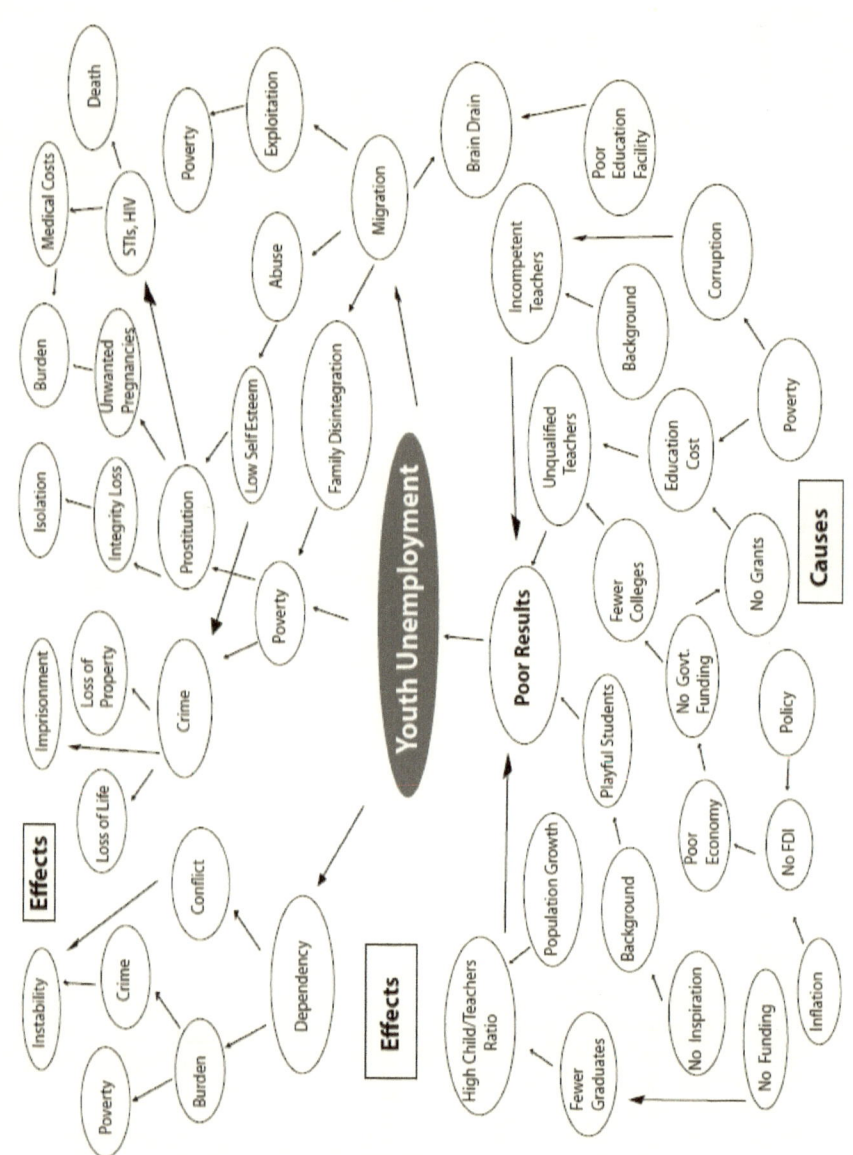

Figure 19: Youth Unemployment

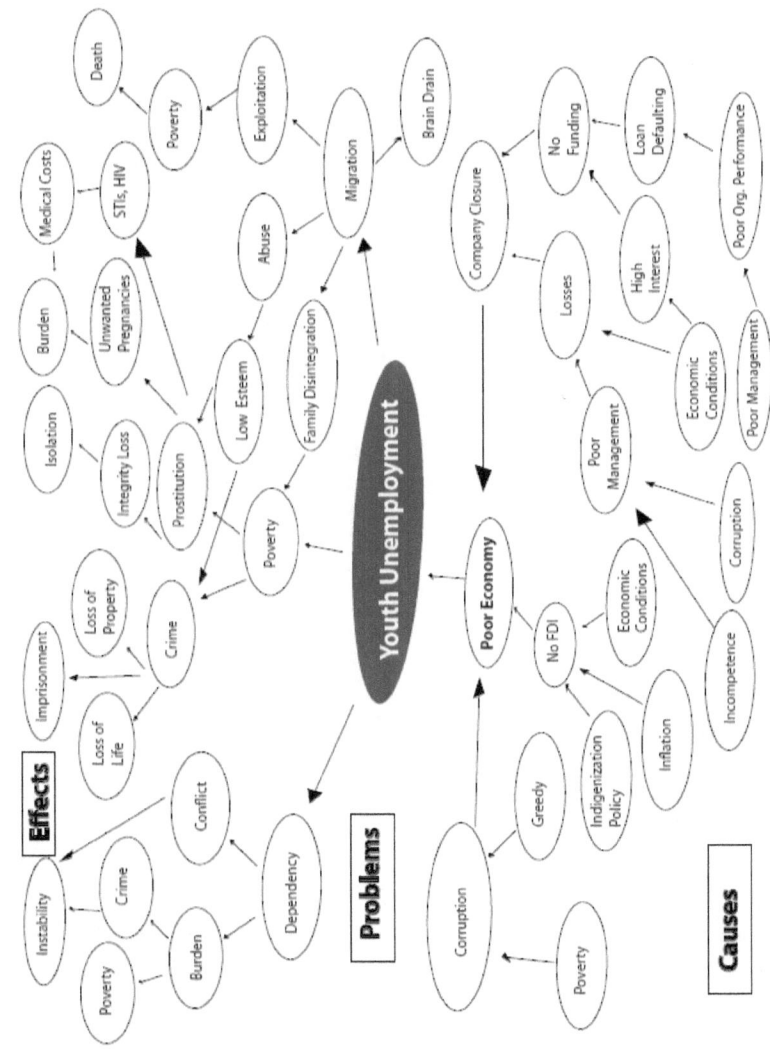

Figure 20: Cause of Youth Unemployment

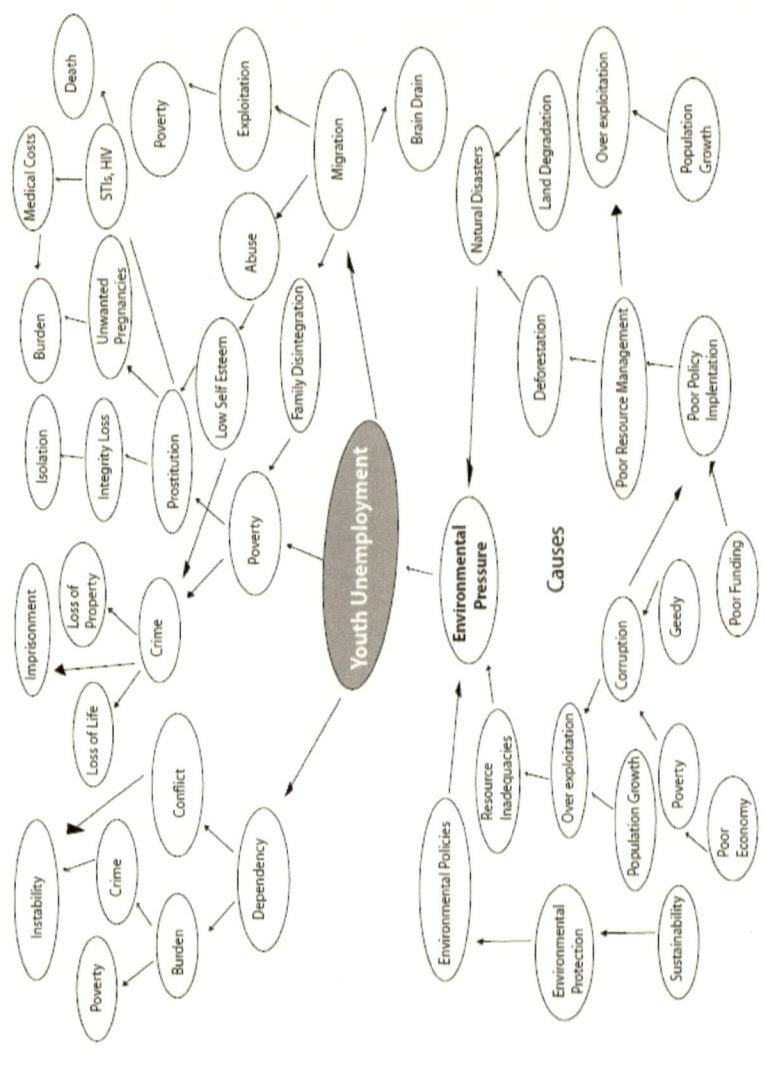

4.8 Clarifying the Problem Using Goals

One can also design a fact-based problem by operationalizing the problem into what will be achieved if the problem was resolved. This is done by stating the policy goals. Policy goals at this point help us figure out and connect whether long-term problems have been properly identified. One then can we see the connection between the policy goal and our conceptualization of the problem.

4.8.1 Clarifying a Policy Problem Using Objectives

We can also improve on our understanding of the policy problem by having a better understanding of the purpose of our effort. This is basically a demand-driven approach to problem solving. We have seen above that the policy goals are what the adopted policy should accomplish. Hence goals are broad, formal, long-term problem-solving achievements that are desired. If it is difficult to connect goals to problems, then one can go down in abstraction by operationalizing goals into policy objectives and then work backward to see if the objectives have a good fit with the problem we have already stated, i.e., the policy goal.

The process involves translating goals into objectives. Usually objectives are more concrete statements about desired end states, with timetables, targets, and populations to be affected. The specific objectives are taken to be the policy problems that need to be sorted out by a policy intervention. Objectives can even be refined by coming up with measurement criteria. These criteria can also be used to compare how close different proposed policy alternatives will come to meeting the goals of solving the problem. During the designing of Policy objectives make sure that they are always SMART. This acronym stands for the following:

- Specific

- Measureable

- Achievable

- Realistic/Reasonable

- Time specific

Because policy objectives are SMART, we can easily see if we have a good understanding of the policy problem. The policy goals framework would look as presented in Figure 21.

Figure 21: Goal and Objective Tree

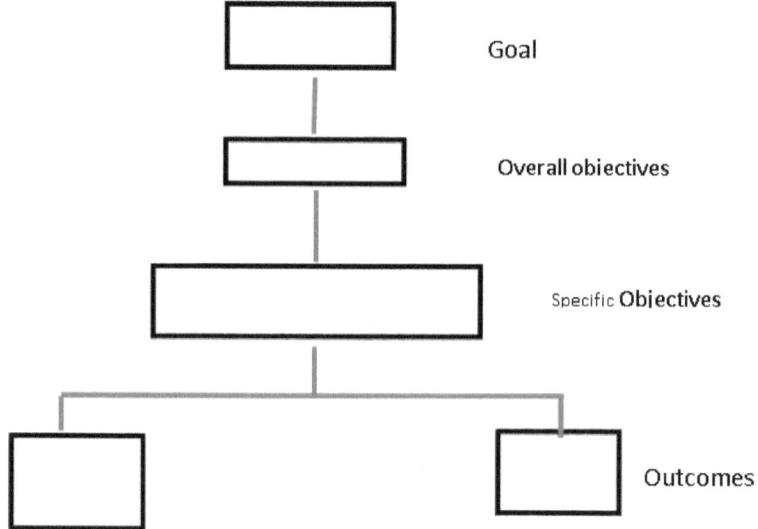

4.8.2 Objectives

Objectives are stated as the desired future situation. In the objective tree the cause-effect relationships we used in the problem tree are transformed into means and ends relationships.

Below is an illustration of how to turn problem statements into objectives:

<u>Problems into Objectives</u>

<u>Problem</u>	<u>Objective</u>
✓ Unclear and inadequate legislation for HIV/AIDS	✓ Amount of legislation for HIV/AIDS put in place
✓ Technical education system does not provide professionals required by the labor market	✓ Contribute to the reform of technical education, which reflect the requirements of the labor market
✓ No system of training in HIV/AIDS management at university levels.	✓ To create a system of training in HIV/AIDS management at university level.

The ITC presents another good illustration of how to develop a problem tree for international traders:

Problem Tree Example: Low Growth in Agricultural Exports

Figure 22: Low Growth in Agriculture Exports

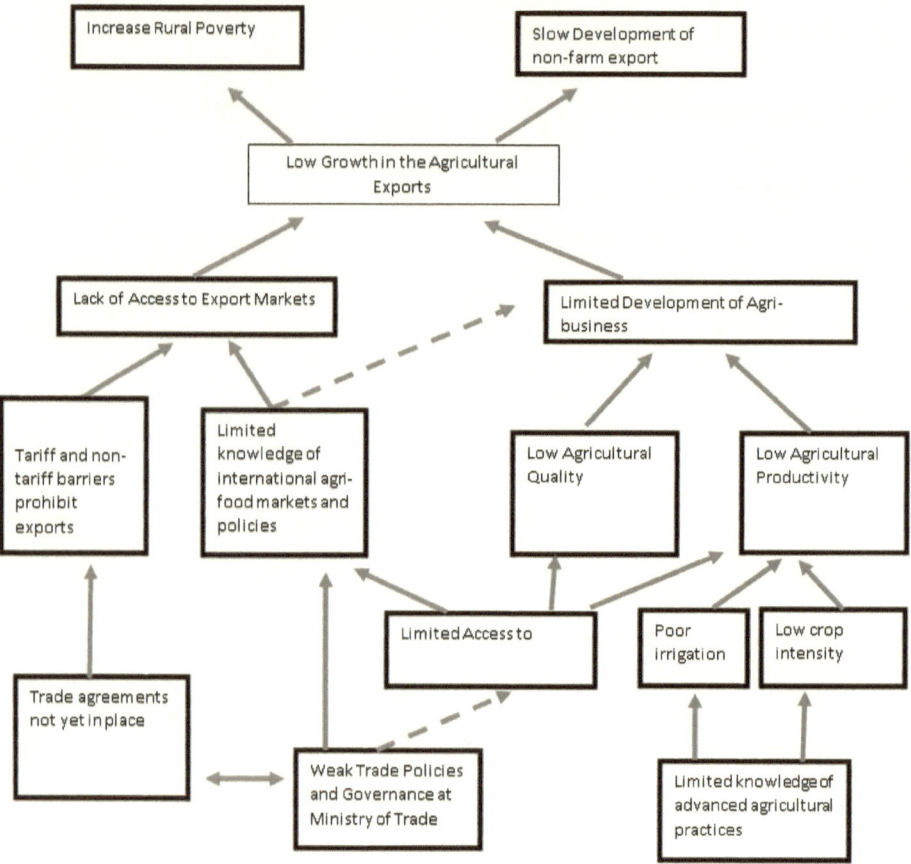

ITC RBM Tools and Guide P.21

The above illustration shows how the major policy problem is identified in order to identify appropriate solutions. At this stage the policy analyst considers the negative conditions seen in connection with the policy problems. The policy analyst then arranges the problems according to cause-effect relationship.

4.8.2.1 How to Do an Objective Tree

Take the example on the problem tree in, which the central problem was "low export diversification." The objective was phrased as "heightened export diversification." One of the low export problem's direct causes can be "absence of value-added industries and products." This can be changed to the objective "increased value-added industries and products." The problem of "scarcity of qualified entrepreneurs and artisans" was caused by "inadequate vocational training." This can become the goal of "New vocational training established."[3]

Using the objective tree, the policy analyst turns what were causes into means and what were effects into ends.

Figure 23: Examples of Objective Tree for Export Diversification

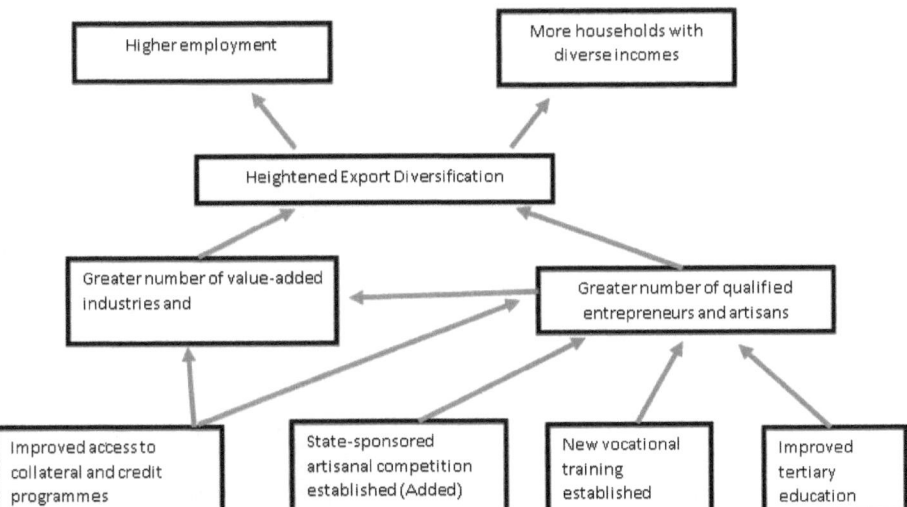

Source: ITC result-based management Guide and Tool Kit P.22

---

[3] http://www.intracen.org/uploadedFiles/intracenorg/Content/About_ITC/Where_are_we_working/Multi-country_programmes/Pact_II/RBM%20Tools%20and%20Guide-Fev%202011-FINAL.pdf

CHAPTER 5

Policy Stakeholders in the Policy Process

5.1 Stakeholder Identification, Analysis, and Management

Who is a policy stakeholder?

A useful definition of a policy stakeholder is "a group or person who has interests that may be affected by a policy initiative or who can influence the definition of that policy."

How can we classify stakeholders?

Several techniques have been used to classify policy stakeholders.

RACI Technique

The RACI technique has been useful as it helps the policy analyst clarify stakeholders according to their roles and responsibility in the context of the policy being designed (www.racitraining.com, April 2014).

The acronym RACI stands for the following:

- Responsibility

- Accountability

- Consulted

- Informed

"Responsibility" involves a situation where the stakeholders will perform policy activities themselves. "Accountability" denotes when the stakeholder is accountable for results of the policy activities. "Consulted" applies when the stakeholder needs to be asked for an opinion on the policy objectives, assumptions, or methods for developing the policy due to his/her expertise or position in the organization. "Informed" signifies policy stakeholders who need to be notified of the outcomes of the policy decisions. This is a tool of involvement from being informed to taking responsibility for the results. However, in real life it is possible for a stakeholder to fall into more than one of these categories.

5.2 Working with RACI Technique

The policy analyst needs to create a working table in order to understand the various qualities of each stakeholder. With this table like one below we can get the possible categories where to place each stakeholder.

Table 4: Stakeholder Mapping

Stakeholder	R	A	C	I	Total
A					
B					
C					
D					

Source: Adapted from www.Racitraining.com2014

The Steps to Create RACI

A number of steps should be followed to construct a good picture of stakeholder details. Below are the major steps in working with RACI.

Step 1

Identify stakeholders on the policy issue at hand through issue analyzing or brainstorming. A list will be compiled. You will find that some stakeholders may be institutions, persons, or groups of individuals. You need therefore to agree at what level of aggregation you want to present the stakeholders.

Step 2

For each stakeholder assign a score on the RACI scheme by using a scoring scale, for example:

Responsibility: 0   (not responsible) to 5(very responsible)

Accountable: 0   (not accountable) to 5 (very accountable)

Consulted   0   (not to be consulted) to 5 (needs to be consulted)

Informed   0   (not to be informed) to 5 (needs to be informed)

This Likert type scale can help the policy analyst to place each stakeholder on the scale of 0 to 5 on each item of the RACI.

Step 3

The policy analyst must consider each stakeholder with respect to the presented scales on RACI. It is very useful to be evidence-based when giving the scores. That is, the score should reflect what happens if the stakeholder's behavior is observed. At the end of this step each stakeholder is positioned on the scale on each item on the RACI.

Step 4

During this step the policy analyst must review the outcome on the matrix for each stakeholder as per step 3.

What will eventually appear at this stage is a complex position for each stakeholder. For example, a stakeholder may not be responsible for the results but needs to be consulted, maybe because of his/her expertise or because he/she is a key political player. A stakeholder may not be consulted but may need to be informed because he/she is a key implementer.

Step 5

During this step we need to rank-order the stakeholders or get to understand how each stakeholder can get involved during and after designing a policy.

The policy analyst must also be mindful of the "powerless." These are stakeholders who will neither be consulted nor assessed as accountable or responsible but will be affected by the policy either negatively or positively.

5.3 Power-Interest Technique

A policy analyst can also use the power-interest technique to clarify stakeholders. Power in this sense could mean "the probability that one Actor will be in a position to carry out his own will despite resistance" (Weber 1947), or power may mean "a relationship in, which one actor 'A' can get another Actor 'B', to do something that B could not otherwise have done" (Pfreffer 1981)

Or power "is the ability of those who possess the power to bring about the outcomes they desire" (Salancik and Pfreffer 1974, 3).

Interest: The reflection bases of interest on the forthcoming policy can be complex. However, common practice shows interest can be understood or defined from narrow or broad approaches.

Narrow approach: This defines interest as a "result of having invested some form of capital, human or financial, something of value" or someone who will be placed at risk as a result of a proposed policy (Clarkson 1994).

Broad approach: This is based on the thinking that "the policy can be vitally affected by, or they can vitally affect, almost everyone" (R. Mitchel[et al. 2009). In this regard one talks of levels of interest rather than no interest at all.

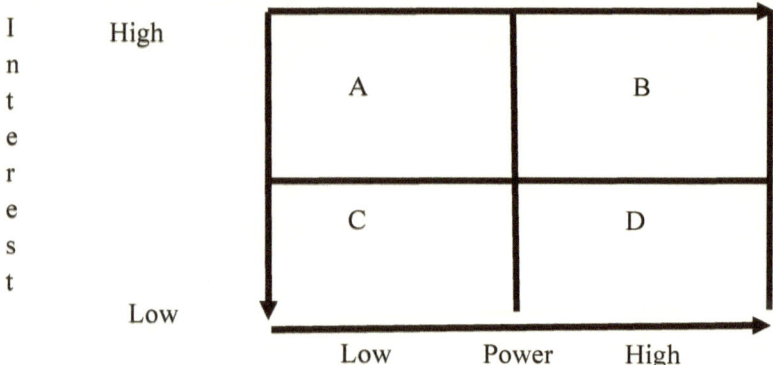

The matrix classifies stakeholders into a minimum of four (4) groups. Quadrant A are those with low power to effect the policy but are very interested in the policy. C are those with low power who have low interest in the issue. D are those who are very powerful but have low interest, and B are those who are very powerful and with very high interested in the issue.

In working with power-interest-technique, the policy analyst must be careful that the policy process is not hijacked by the most powerful and most interested. Similarly, the classification should help the policy analyst to develop a proper policy communication strategy or/and engagement strategy. In most cases the policy analyst may find out that much of the population is in quadrant C (low power–low interest). This group tends to be the disenfranchised or the poor. The challenge is how to "speak truth to power" or for the policy analyst to present the "truth of the powerless."

5.4 Power, Legitimacy, and Urgency Technique

This technique helps the policy analyst clarify the stakeholder's position based on the salience of each stakeholder. The clarification here is based on three factors, namely power, legitimacy, and urgency (R. Mitchell 1997). The stakeholder classes that result from the various combinations of power, urgency, and legitimacy are shown in the figure below:

Figure 24: Stakeholder Classes

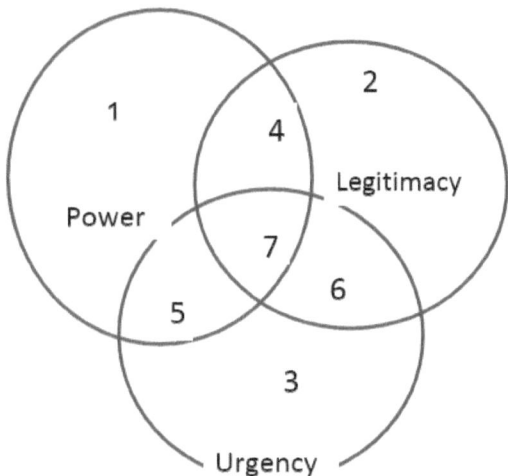

Source: Ronald K. Mitchell et al. "Towards a theory of stakeholder identification and salience." *Academy of Management* 22 October.

We can see the various combinations of legitimacy, power, and urgency. This clarification leads to more complex and interesting stakeholder classes. Mitchell comes up with seven (7) such classes as presented below:

Stakeholder Typology:

The figure shows that when one, two, or three attributes are present, they are able to appreciate the complex roles that stakeholders can play in the policy process.

Figure 25: Stakeholder Identification

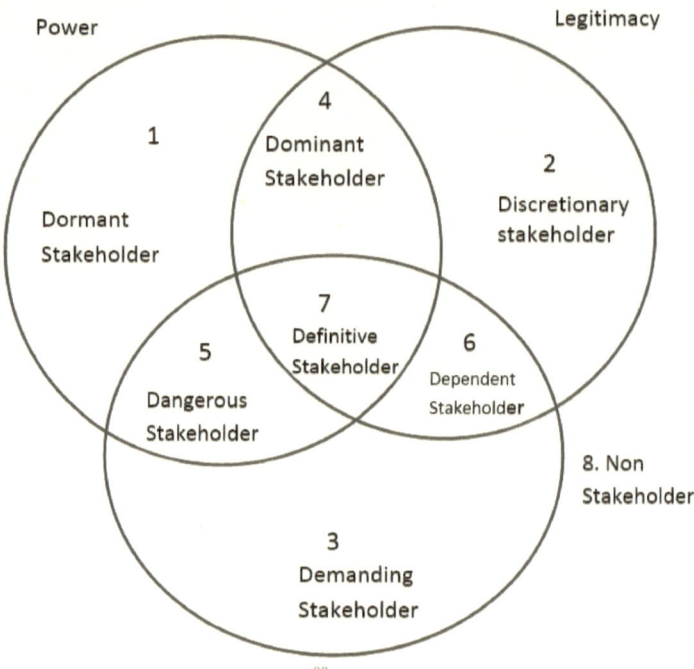

Source: Ronald K. Mitchell, Joe Agle, and Tom Wood. 1997. "Towards a theory of stakeholder identification and salience." *Academy of Management* 22 (4).

The power, legitimacy, and urgency technique, at times also called the salience, each stakeholder will be based upon power, legitimacy, and urgency (World Press 2015). The model presents the following stakeholder groups.

5.4.1 Dormant Stakeholders

These are stakeholders who have power to impose their will on others but have neither legitimacy nor urgency. Ideally the approach by the policy analyst is to always keep them informed on the issues of interest to them.

5.4.2 Discretionary Stakeholders

These are stakeholders who have legitimacy but have neither power nor urgent policy claims. They tend to be the "powerless," the poor who have legitimacy policy claim to the political system or the services provided.

5.4.3 Demanding Stakeholders:

These are stakeholders who have urgent claim on the policy issues, but have no power or legitimacy to enforce those policy claims.

5.4.4 Dominant Stakeholders:

These are stakeholders who have both power and legitimate claims but see issues as urgent.

5.4.5 Dangerous Stakeholders

These are stakeholders who have power and urgent claims but lack legitimacy. They are taken to be dangerous as they often resort to coercion and even violence to achieve their policy claims.

5.4.6 Dependent Stakeholders:

These are stakeholders who have no power but have urgent and legitimate claims.

5.4.7 Definitive Stakeholders:

These are stakeholders who have power, legitimacy, and urgency and therefore need to be communicated with.

5.4.8 Non Stakeholders:

These stakeholders are at times called "non-issue stakeholders." They have no power, no legitimacy, and no urgency. These appear to be beyond the scope of the issue at hand. Depending on the issue, this group of stakeholders may enter the policy dynamism as one of the seven categories mentioned earlier.

5.5 Policy Implications on Stakeholders

Stakeholder analysis can also be used to review the implications of a policy on stakeholders. The table below illustrates how to understand the effect of a "will be policy" on the stakeholders.

In the table below we have a government trying to come up with a policy. This process involves stakeholders like exporters and importers and government ministries such as the Ministry of Industry and Trade. Although all these stakeholders may have an interest in having a national trade policy, they will differ on the perceived problems, the effects of the policy, and the benefits and costs of the envisaged policy.

Table 5: Stakeholder Benefits

Stakeholder	Interest	Problem Perceived	Resources & Mandate	Potential Conflict
Exporters	Efficient, effective access to customers and international markets	– Frequent delays at borders – High export taxes – Inconsistent – Changing export laws applications	Willingness to pay taxes	Frustrated with additional paper work demand by customs procedures
Government Ministry of Trade	Improved Balance of Trade	Lack of rules to properly oversee trade policy; poor exports infrastructure.	Budget for policies of interest to country	Frustration by budget allocated.
Importers	– Efficient and effective clearing procedures – Clear laws on excise duties to be paid on goods	– Frequent delays at clearing ports – Unnecessary and changing penalties – High import taxes.		

Similarly, a policy analyst should know that doing a stakeholder analysis is useful in fulfilling current social and government requirements for policy engagement. Many governments now require that any policy process shows "who was consulted and how." Policy stakeholder analysis is therefore not a "by-the-way" approach but is now at the center of any democratic policy process and good governance.

5.6 Policy Stakeholders' Engagement

The policy process is an interrelated process with several unique phases when it comes to stakeholder engagement. The phases include

i) pre-policy phase;

ii) policy design phase;

iii) policy approval phase; and

iv) policy implementation.

It may be unusual to find that some stakeholder plays a part in all these phases. But some stakeholders may only be more involved at pre-policy phase. For the latter they provide input to agenda setting, miss out the policy design phase, but may appear again during policy implementation. Depending on the type of policy, some stakeholders may be more dominant at approval phase but not implementation.

This dynamic process creates challenges for policy analysts, as they need to understand and define "engagement." The question is "Does engagement mean consultation? Or does it mean full ownership in all the four phases?"

CHAPTER 6

Policy Future

After the policy problem is defined, analysts must move into looking for options solutions on how to resolve the policy problem. Best practices show that before policy choices are made, it is important to also shift our thoughts into the future dimension of such problems. The job of a policy analyst therefore is to consider the probable, the plausible, and the very unlikely futures in order to challenge assumptions on the policy options being considered.

However, the challenge of looking at the future is that there are many ranges of possibilities. At the apex of the curve we have the most likely future based on the correct knowledge and expectations. At the far end is the highly unlikely future based on the unknown knowledge and expectations.

6.1 Types of Future

Possible Future	-	might happen
Plausible Future	-	could happen
Probable Future	-	likely to happen
Preferable Future	-	want to happen

When we look at these "futures", the forces, thinking, and techniques to understand them differ. The table below is an illustration of considerations required when working with "futures":

Table 6: Probable and Plausible Future

Type of Futures	Forces	Thinking	Techniques
Probable	Constant trends	Definite; scientific	Historical extrapolation
Plausible	Discontinuous; surprises	Speculative imagination	Scenarios; simulation

6.2 The Future Way

Traditional thinking about the future has always tended to follow the "inside-out approaches." In such approaches, policy making is taken to be a rational approach. It always thought that policy analysis is about examining the organization and forming the inside-out. The policy analyst is supposed to position the organization in the environment. The outside environment is taken to be there to manage or take opportunity out of it. In such a rational approach; inside-out policy analysis involves predicting the future of the current organization setup.

The reality of policy analysis, however, shows that the "inside-out" is one side of a complex organization story. The policy analyst should create stories about relevant issues-outside the environment of the organization that might evolve in the future. But a policy analyst should always stretch his/her thinking about opportunities and threats when making strategic policy choices. In this regard policy analysis calls for "outside-in" thinking too. The information from both inside-out and outside-in must form the basis for a good scenario development.

6.3 Scenario-Way

The scenario-way of thinking begins by the policy analyst identifying the forces of change—e.g., economic, political, legal, social, or technological—and then using that information to inform strategic policies. Most important, this helps improve the policy analyst's capability to contribute to better decisions for now and the future. The challenge of the policy analyst, as Pierre Wack said, is to "get inside the minds of decision makers in order to affect strategic decisions. They should create a scenario to paint vivid and diverse pictures of the future so that policy makers may rehearse the implications of these factors for their organization (P. Wack 1985)

6.3.1 Scenario-Way Thinking Process

There are many frameworks for scenario thinking. The simplest is presented in the figure below:

Figure 26: Scenario Driving Forces

In the figure above, immediate driving forces would include the organization's immediate forces for change: customer base, competitors, partners, the community, and so on. The contextual driving forces include such forces as the political, economic, and technical, which are broad in nature. In thinking about policy, we therefore think about the contextual and immediate forces.

In this approach, only after the Policy Analyst has designed scenarios about the external environment can they consider implications of such to their organization or issue. That is why outside-in thinking is so important because it takes the policy analysts out of their reality and makes policies as future anticipators and an exercise of future risk management.

Also the policy analyst needs to be aware that in policy futures, not all "problems" need to be resolved by policies. Some of the policy problems may just be resolved administratively. For example, most issues, which arise when implementers follow the proper governance procedures or rules would require an administrative refinement rather than policy changes. It is important then not to confuse policy problems with implementation problems. Future thinking methodologies have been useful tools in this regard.

There are many tools for looking forward. These can help us address discontinuity and uncertainties. They can also help us design robust policies that withstand the test of times (E. E. A 2011). Let us review some of these common methods.

6.4 Foresight Methodologies

Foresight exercises are becoming useful methodologies in helping design an efficient and effective policy logic. The rationale for understanding a foresight exercise may be quite complex, but generally, "Foresight is not only about analyzing or dreaming about the policy future but supporting Policy Analysts to actively shape the future" (JRC2013.1).

When we work with foresight exercises, "we assume that the future is not predetermined." We assume that the future can be shaped by the choices we make today. However, foresight is not forecasting. It is not planning. It does not define policy. Foresight only helps us to inform decision making by making us aware of the future development and how this may interact with the policies we make today. A good foresight result must then be fed into policy making (EU 2013).

At this stage of policy development, the functions of foresight can be summed up and described in the six specific functions, as done by JRC (2013.1)

6.4.1 Functions of Foresight

- Informing policy: By generating insights regarding the dynamics of change, future challenges and options, along with new ideas and transmitting them to policymakers as an input to policy conceptualizations and design.

- Facilitating policy implementation: By enhancing the capacity for change within a given policy field through building a common awareness of the current situation and future challenges, as well as new networks and visions among stakeholders.

- Embedding participation in policy-making: By facilitating the participation of civil society in the policy-making process, thereby improving its transparency and legitimacy.

- Supporting policy definition: By jointly translating outcomes from the collective process into specific options for policy definition and implementation.

- Reconfiguring the policy-system: In a way that makes it more apt to address long-term challenges.

- Symbolic function: indicating to the public that policy is based on rational information (JRC 2013; EC 2015; P. Des-Meodt 2005).

6.4.1.1 Illustration Using Foresight

The methodological framework in using foresight can be from simple to complex sequences.

Step 1

We need to understand where the organization is now.

Step 2

Foresight what could happen by a particular time.

Step 3

Decision making on what should be done to reach or change that future.

The best practice is to avoid thinking that the process is a sequence when it should be understood that the steps are interlinked and can take place in parallel. The process is always interactive with feedback loops (Europe 2013).

6.5 Scenario Thinking

Scenarios help the policy analyst to think about the future dimension of the policy problems and its implications.

A scenario such as this begins when the policy analyst asks "What would happen if such-and-such occurs?" For example, "What would happen if the work week were increased to six days?" Once such a question is asked, the policy analyst may start seeing or indeed visioning various outcomes of such a policy decision. "Fundamentally, Scenarios help ordering our minds about alternative futures in, which today's decisions may play out" (Rutgers.edu 2015). Scenarios may also assist the policy analyst to be aware of potential problems that might occur if the policy analyst was to make the proposed policy option. Organizations find that such an understanding could help them decide to take precautions to minimize the risks that may come when such risks are unmanageable. In general terms, scenarios can help the organization by

- building understanding of the broader operating environment;

- helping embrace and structure uncertainty;

- creating a vocabulary about the future and identify alternative futures;

- making key assumptions explicit and surface hidden risks; and

- providing a context for developing and testing strategic options or policies.

6.6 Think about the Future

There are several ways of thinking about the future and its implication on policy problems. First is what is called "Future forward" and second, "Future backward."

Future forward approaches involve a type of reasoning that starts with the current world and then creates the story for some "Future." Such a story is usually based on some historical logic.

Future backward is based on first describing a desired Future and then exploring options to reach that Future. In some studies, this approach is called Back-casting. That is a method in, which the future desired conditions are envisioned, and steps are then defined to attain those conditions.

In some studies, these two approaches have been called "explorative" and "normative" scenarios (EEA 2011). With explorative scenarios we explore the possible effects of specific measures (policy changes) on future developments. By contrast, with normative scenarios we are finding ways of reaching specified goals (EEA 2011) or testing alternative policy options to see how efficient or effective they are (EEA 2011; PBL 2010).

6.6.1 Common Steps in Building Scenarios

When building scenarios, there are some important steps to follow. Below are some useful steps.

Step 1

6.6.1.1 Focal Issues or Questions

The beginning of "thinking" is guided by "focal issues of decision."

That is, What do you as a policy analyst want to know about the "future"? What are the key factors you would like to know about the future that will Impact on the effectiveness and efficiency of your policy choice?

At this step it is also useful to specify the appropriate time horizon for the scenarios you want to build. This specification of time helps as a means for strategic policy decisions.

Step 2

6.6.1.2 Key Forces Identification

In this step we identify the key forces in the environment and the drivers that will influence the identified forces. Usually these forces and drivers are identified at Macro and Micro environment levels. Key micro forces have a direct influence on the issue; for example, if you are dealing with the future of a specific manufacturing industry, micro drivers can be related to the sector market trends, specific regulations on manufacturing, new techniques, etc.

Macro key forces are broader, possibly global, forces that relate to social, policy, economic, and environment futures that might have an impact on the issue being considered. From macro forces one can build a model of the relevant "environment" that will include critical trends and forces. From this one can then map out the cause-effect relationship among these forces. There will be many macro forces, but it is advisable to always identify trends and uncertainties, which are important in determining the key decision factors.

At this stage, two key questions will assist the analysis of macro factors:

1. What factors will influence the focal issue or decision?

2. What will policymakers want to know when making their policy choices?

Step 3

6.6.1.3 Rank Driving Forces

At this step the policy analyst should rank the key forces and driving forces by "degree of importance" and "degree of uncertainty." This is usually done by making an *XY* plot with importance versus uncertainty elements.

In the diagram below those key forces or driving forces that fall in the quadrant of high importance and high uncertainty should be looked at carefully, as they are most critical to providing different scenarios that may be important. One can select a number of such scenarios for further study.

Table 7: Importance/Uncertainty Matrix

Importance		Low	Medium	High
	High	G	H	I
	Medium	D	E	F
	Low	A	B	C
		Low	Medium	High
			Uncertainty	

Outcome of Sorting

From the diagram we can sort out to extreme combinations:

High importance/high uncertainties,

These driving forces are potential shapers of different futures for, which the organization's longer-term planning should prepare.

Step 4

6.6.1.4 Selecting Scenario Logic

Results from step 3, the ranking exercise, will help identify and define the key variables for building scenarios. That is, ranking helps identify the axis around, which the scenarios can be constructed. The approach is to "flesh out skeletal scenarios" by looking at the key factors and driving forces developed in the earlier steps, especially steps 1 and 2.

One technique is to have each key factor and driving force given some vote in the scenarios. For example, if we have two driving forces, this leads to four possible combinations that can be built into a narrative about the scenarios. The success of this exercise will be based on developing internally consistent "story lines" by creating both desirable and undesirable futures within the different scenarios. It makes sense to pay attention to the high importance/low uncertainty and high importance/high uncertainty quadrants of the matrix.

Step 5

6.6.1.5 Implications of Scenarios

Once the scenarios are defined, we then need to look for their implications. Some key questions need to be answered at this point: "What could happen if the different possibilities occur? What are the strategic implications of the scenarios for the particular decision we selected at step 1? What are the key elements of policy framework stemming from the scenarios? What would be the best policy options in relation to each element?"

Step 6

6.6.1.6 Opportunities and Threats Assessments

The sixth stage involves risk management. We need to examine each scenario crafted in detail to determine the opportunities and threats that each poses in the organization. We need to find out if these opportunities and threats are common to all the scenarios. Is the organization prepared to seize opportunities and minimize threats?

6.7 Practical Tools to Work with Scenarios

Below we discuss practical ways to work with the six steps.

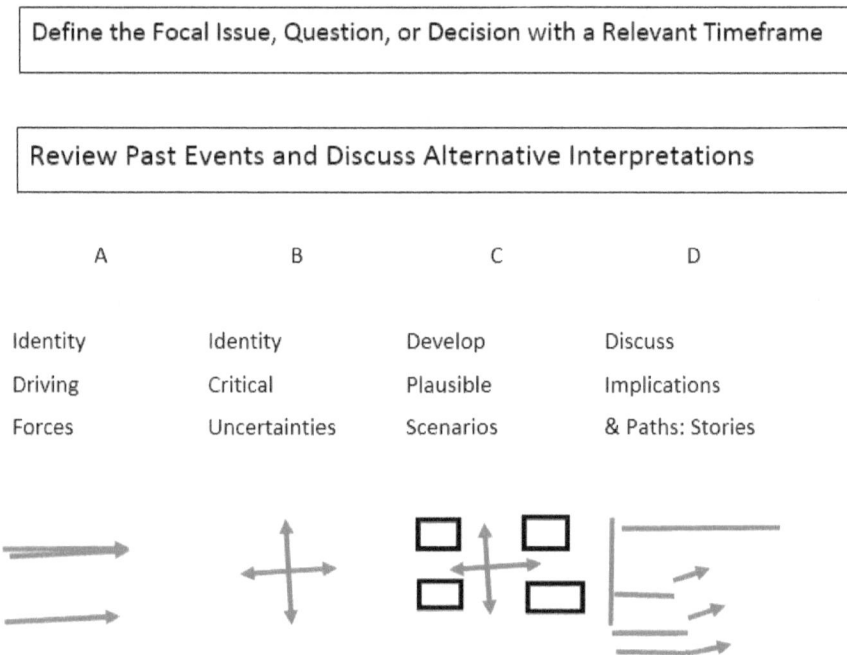

	Define the Focal Issue, Question, or Decision with a Relevant Timeframe

	Review Past Events and Discuss Alternative Interpretations

A	B	C	D
Identity Driving Forces	Identity Critical Uncertainties	Develop Plausible Scenarios	Discuss Implications & Paths: Stories

6.8 Approaches to Designing a Scenario

Best practices from the six steps above teach us that it is important to clarify the purpose of the exercise of building the scenario, given the different objectives that scenarios intend to achieve. So we need to agree on how our scenario will be used. Also all participants in the exercise should understand the key question of the scenario. The key question drives the brainstorming.

6.8.1 Examples of Key Questions

- What will the future of the country/region/organization look like in 2020? We can even create narrow questions, e.g., what will be the level of productivity in the organization by 2020?

- What risks do we face in the organization for the next ten years? What contingency plans should we put in place to mitigate such risks? This question is purely a risk management focus.

- What policy should the organization adopt in order to achieve outcome (Y) by 2020? This question will be a policy development focus.

- How robust is policy Y or program Y, over a ten-year timeframe (in the light of Z)? This is more of a policy or program review focus.

- What should be the goal of organization X, and how should it be achieved over the next ten years? This again is a vision focus question.

6.8.2 General Comments

In all cases the policy analyst must know that it is possible to formulate the purpose of the scenarios to work as a question. Also the analyst's thoughts should always be driven by how the scenarios will be used in practice. For instance, are we building scenarios to help generate dialogue around possible risks and priorities in a particular country/regional organization? Or are our scenarios going to be used to develop "early warning" indicators that will be monitored regularly by managers of that organization? Or will the scenarios be used to test a range of policy options that have already been developed?

6.8.3 Scenarios in Time

When developing scenarios, the issue of time horizon must be handled. Of course there are no hard and fast rules. However, the best practices call for reflecting the question being examined.

6.8.4 Common Simple Rules Show the Following:

- Work should focus on narrowly defined trends and drivers; e.g., the national political situation: this can be reduced to three to five years.

- Where scenarios are used to test robustness of existing policy, they should look twice as far; for example, scenario to test a three-year medium-term expenditure plan should look at least six years ahead.

- Scenarios on such issues as climate change tend to have a longer time frame, even fifty years (EEA 2011).

CHAPTER 7

Methodologies in Designing Scenarios

There are three major methodologies in working with scenarios in policy making:

- "Two Axes" method

- "Branch Analysis" method

- "Cone of Plausibility" method

7.1 The Two Axes Method

Using this method, we can develop scenarios that are illustrative rather than predictive. The product of this method is particularly suited to testing medium- to long-term policy direction by ensuring it is robust in a range of environments.

Scenarios designed using this method focus on a time period beyond ten to twenty years in the future.

7.2 The Branch Analysis Method

This method is suited to developing scenarios around specific turning-points that are known in advance—for example, turning points after an election, referendum, or peace process agreement. For example, we need to rethink on policies after the election of Mr. D. Trump in America. This approach works best for a shorter time horizon, generally up to five years.

7.3 The Cone of Plausibility Method

The cone of plausibility defines futures that might reasonably occur:

- Determine questions and time horizon.

- Identify drivers, trends, and potential events relevant to the scope and question.

- Identify principal clusters of drivers that have the highest impact and are the most uncertain.

- Prioritize clusters to identify the drivers that have the highest impact and are the most uncertain.

- Based on the prioritization, select two scenario axes that generate four relevant scenario quadrants.

- Develop the scenarios into stories or narratives.

- Once the scenario narratives have been produced, then identify specific points during the time leading up to those scenarios, which may then be monitored as indicators whether events are unfolding in a way that is consistent with the scenario.

7.4 Example of Using Two Axes Method

7.4.1 Issue: Market Integration in Africa

The group brainstorms a long list of forces that they believe could shape the future of Africa's common market.

Issues of uncertainty may arise—e.g., access to global markets, limited access to technology, leadership, and citizen attitudes to integration. It can also be seen that major demographic shifts, in particular the increasing movement of people (skilled and unskilled) within Africa and the growing youth population, are going to be predetermined forces for change for the next generation in Africa.

From the above analysis we have sample list of critical contrasting uncertainties:

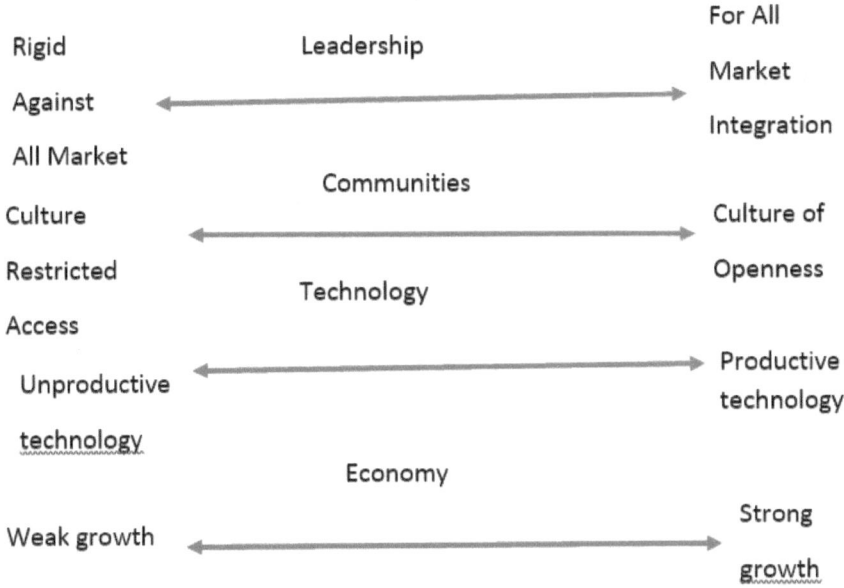

The approach is to clarify the nature of these critical uncertainties by trying to brainstorm the polar ways in, which these uncertainties could play out.

7.4.2 Crossing Combination

Since the future is not one uncertainty at a time, the group involved in scenario development needs to come up with different combinations of these "axes of uncertainty" to create a scenario framework (D. Sceare 2004). The "axes of uncertainty," as they are sometimes called, represent a continuum of possibility ranging between two extremes. For example, uncertainty about the role of devolution in Africa can be presented by one axis:

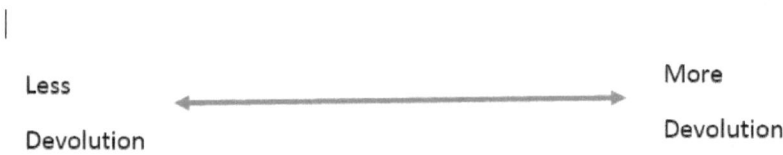

And we could consider another uncertainty, the future role of the economy:

Then we cross the two axes to create a framework, which can then be used to explore four possible scenarios for the future. This is what is called the scenario matrix:

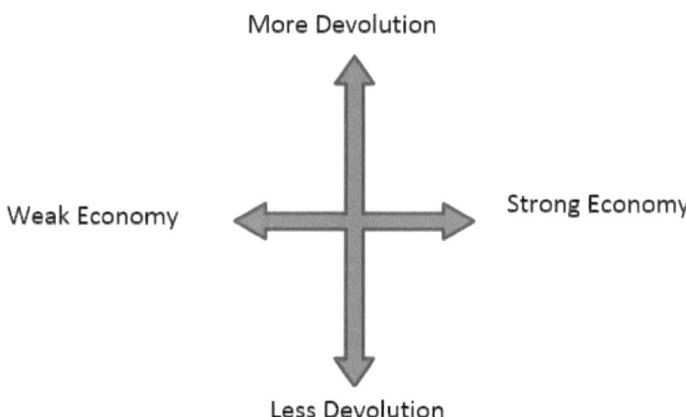

After creating a scenario framework, we can then develop scenarios into narrative, stories, which begin in the present and end in the future. A good scenario should help the organization learn, adapt, and take effective policy actions.

To use scenario stories in policy formulation, one should just imagine living and working in each of the scenarios. The key question to ask is "What if this scenario is the future? Do the actions we would take today to prepare the scenario implications highlight any strategic policy choices that we need to address?" The scenario implications are the building blocks of the organization strategic policies.

At the end of this exercise, a number of uncertainties may have to be reexamined, combined, and at times split to avoid too many or too few scenarios. For example, the uncertainty called "resources" may be used to combine human and nonhuman resources. Depending on the question, combining these two may be problematic. This is because uncertainty regarding financial versus human capacity may be dealt with differently. Also "culture" needs to be defined as it may mean religion, community, concerns, and so on.

After the uncertainties are clarified, the scenario building group need to create the scenario matrix, as illustrated below:

All Market Integration Matrix for Africa:

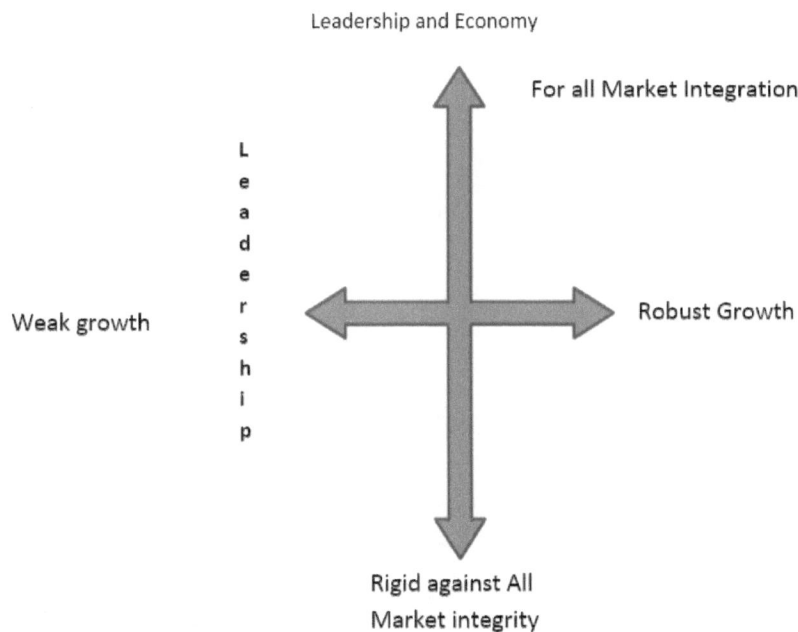

Resources and Culture

Resources and Culture

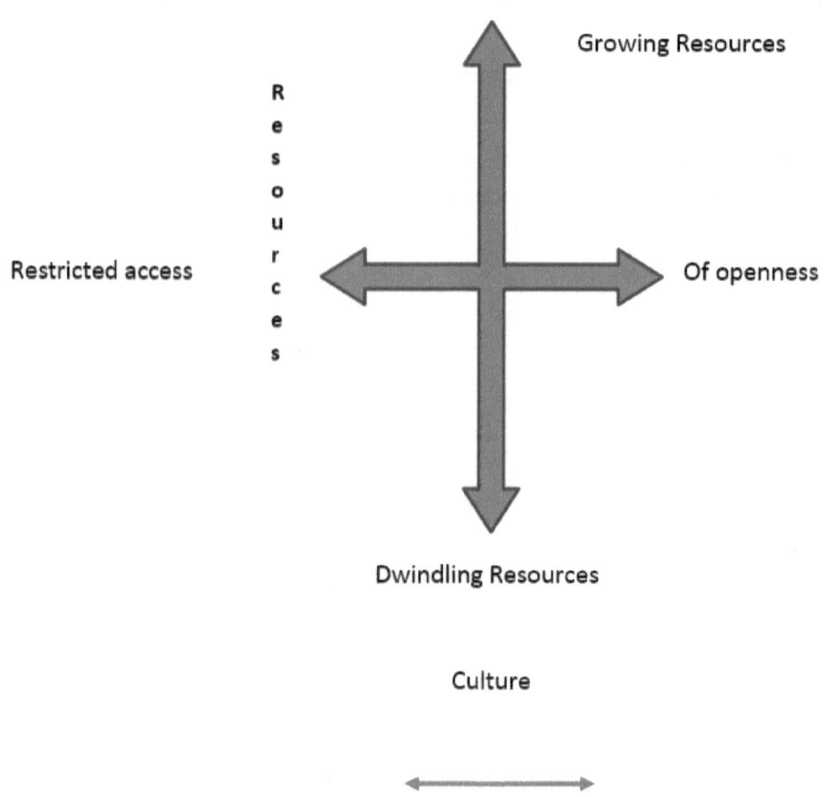

Growing Resources

Restricted access

Of openness

Dwindling Resources

Culture

Figure 27: Illustration of Two Axes Method on SABCO Integration

Very fast economic growth

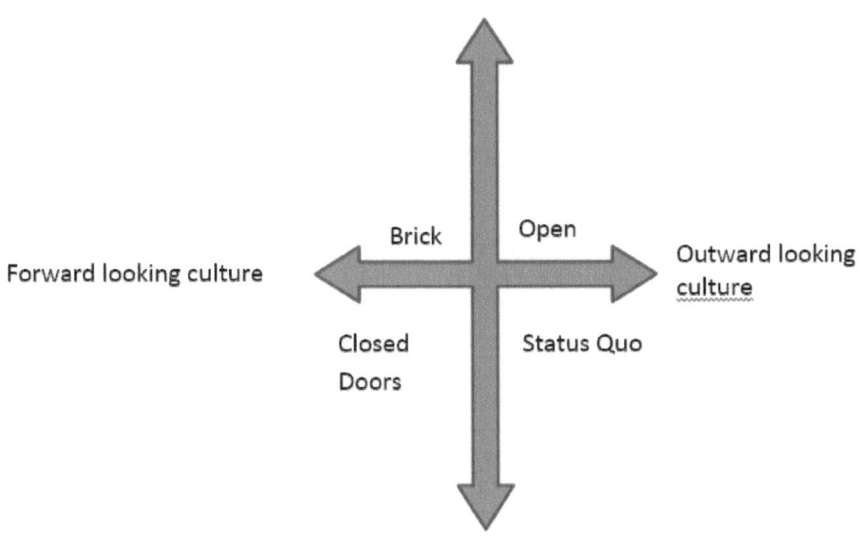

The scenario building group needs to try crossing as many combinations as possible of the axes of uncertainty to be able to create a useful scenarios framework. This effort will produce some very exciting matrices. At this point the group should develop and write "narratives" that seem to tell the "story" of how far each matrix, each "different world," could evolve over the next twenty years for African market integration.

At this stage, the group should focus on each market integration scenario and imagine the opportunities and challenges for African Common Market Integration in that world. It is important for the group to assume that *future* is indeed a reality and then consider how the scenario might positively impact the African Common Market for the next twenty years.

7.4.3 Conclusion

The two axes method is excellent in presenting a rich picture of multiple facets of potential futures if done properly. However, to ensure that the scenarios produced are credible, one needs to draw on well-documented evidence and analysis and review final scenarios for coherence and internal consistency.

7.5 Branch Analysis Method

Using the Branch Analysis Method

Branch analysis is used to develop a range of potential futures. As in the two axes method, the policy analysis should start with the top-level question. Then important events are identified in a systematic sequence, and potential consequences are mapped into a branching diagram. Then contrasting scenarios are developed using this branching approach.

7.5.1 Five Stages in Using the Branch Analysis Method

Step 1

The policy analyst determines the question and time frame. To place the question, like in two axes method, the question needs to be "SMART."

Step 2

Identify drivers, trends, and key events relevant to the question.

Step 3

Select a limited number of key events and potential outcomes.

Step 4

Build branch diagram based on key events and potential outcomes of each event.

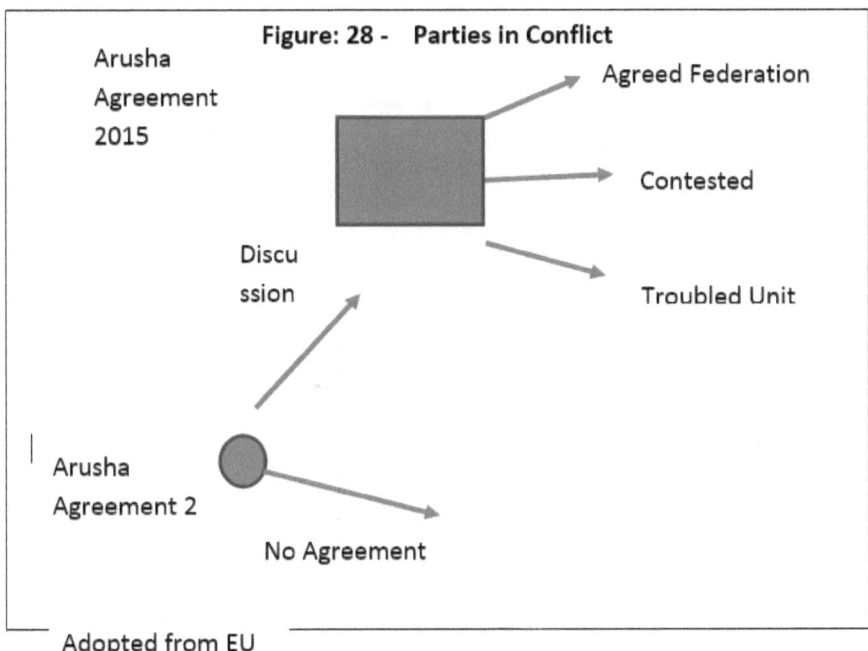

Figure: 28 - **Parties in Conflict**

Arusha Agreement 2015

Agreed Federation

Contested

Discussion

Troubled Unit

Arusha Agreement 2

No Agreement

Adopted from EU

Step 5

Identify scenario spaces based on distinct plausible outcomes. Develop characteristics for each of the scenarios

Step 6

Develop the scenarios into stories or narratives.

Example:

Figure 29: Three scenarios for Country x 2030 Based on 3 drivers and 3 assumptions

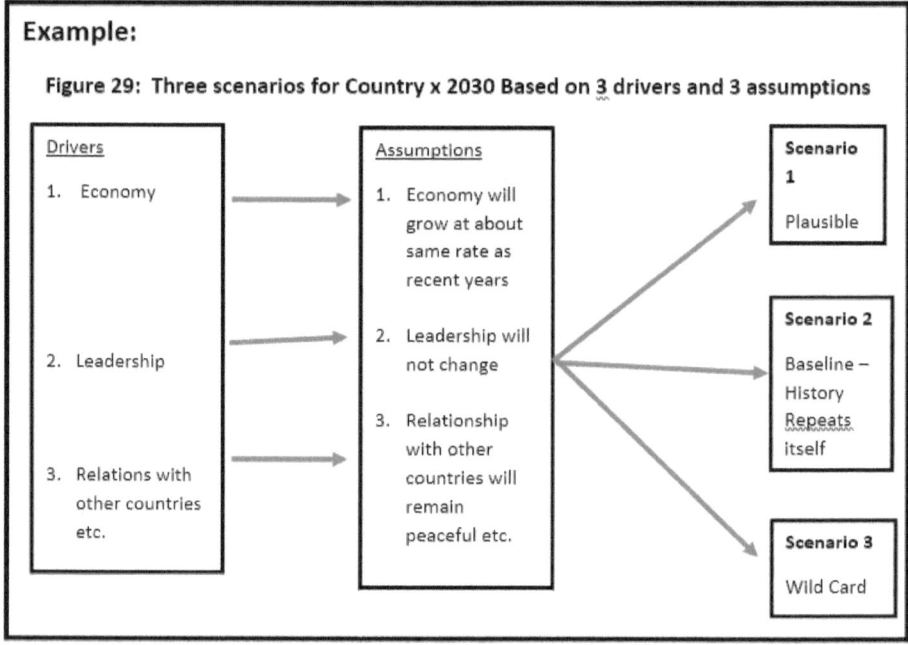

7.6 Cone of Plausibility Method

Process

In using a cone of plausibility method, several steps need to be followed to create scenarios:

- A range of scenarios are developed from a series of identified drivers and assumptions.

- The scenarios are based on the most likely pathways as well as the more extreme or less likely future pathways.

The method can be used to look at short-, medium-, or long-term futures but is most often suited to short time horizons. Generally, however, the plausibility method enables the analyst to produce a clear and robust audit trail toward each scenario while presenting the evidence base throughout.

7.6.1 Key Components of the Process

When developing cone of plausibility, we need to determine the key question and working time frame.

Identify drivers and trends relevant to the question based on relevant research and analysis, and determine the behavior of each driver to produce a corresponding list of assumptions. One approach is to have create or have one assumption per driver. For each of the drivers, generate a baseline scenario based on the initial set of drivers and assumptions. The baseline is usually a simple projection of the current situation. If we change one or more of the assumptions, we can generate corresponding alternative scenarios. Then we need to consider the impact that the change(s) would have on the baseline and change it accordingly. Then we can repeat this step where appropriate to generate further alternative scenarios.

We can also radically change at least two of the assumptions to generate a more extreme scenario (wild card). This is likely to be high-impact and low-probability. Then after these changes, we can develop a narrative incorporating specific events where relevant.

7.6.2 Example Using Cone of Plausibility Method

We can imagine potential futures as a cone radiating out from the present (CFM 2010).

Figure 30: The Futures Cone

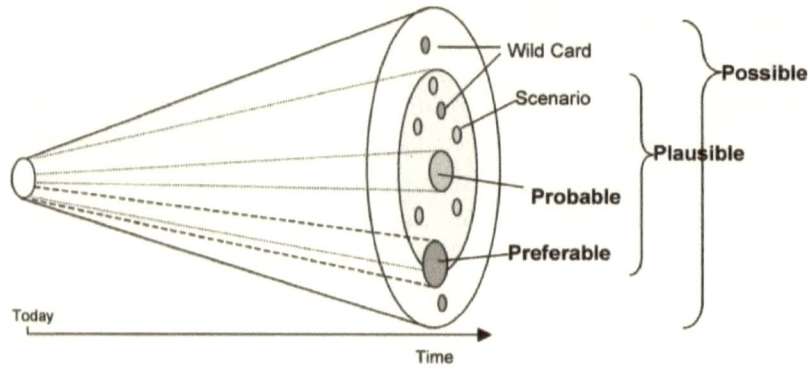

Figure 31: Limits of Plausibility

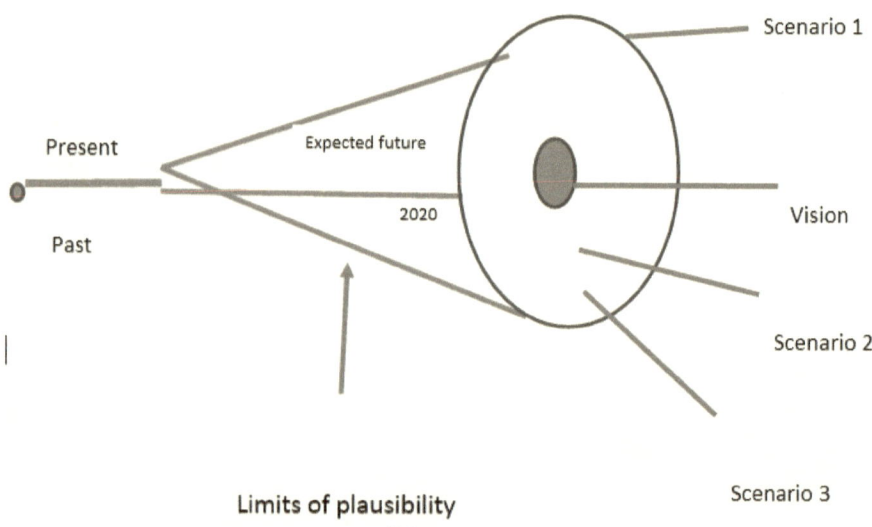

The edges of the cone are defined by the limits of plausibility (CFM 2010). "The dead center in the cone of plausibility is the expected future. This is how the future would look if business proceeds as usual." In most cases, however, when thinking about the future, one has to be careful, as the most expected future is usually highly unlikely.

Oftentimes it is probable that many "environmental" forces will cause the organization to move away from that course to elsewhere. Usually the landing pad will be found in between the expected future and the limits of plausibility (CFM 2010; WFS 2008; Conway 2003).

CHAPTER 8

Future Wheel Methodology

There are concerns identifying the impact of policy during the policy design phase. "Policy consequence" analysis is therefore necessary before policy choices. We usually use the future wheel methodology if we want to explore the full impact of any policy change. It is hard to identify all possible outcomes. Green (1972) said usually people only list the first consequence that they recognize and close the thinking quickly, causing errors of the third type (Dunn 1984).

Future wheel is a virtual tool, which offers a way of brainstorming the direct and indirect consequences of a decision. It is also a way of organizing our thinking and questioning about the future. It helps the policy analysis to anticipate the possible consequences as well as possible consequences of any policy change. The hope is to come down from the possible to plausible consequences.

8.1 Process Working with Future Wheel

- One needs to write the change being introduced in the center of a piece of paper.

Figure 32: Future Wheel

- Then we identify first-order consequences, which are possible direct consequences of that change. We write each consequence in a circle and then connect each first-order consequence to the central idea with an arrow.

Figure 33: First-Order Consequences

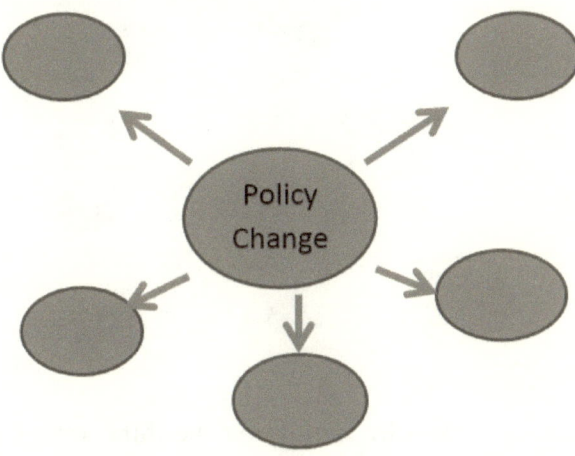

If the policy is introduced, what major consequences can we see?

Second-Order Consequences

- For each first-order consequence, we develop consequences flowing from it. This means identifying indirect, second-order consequences.

Complete the picture by writing all possible second-order consequences out of each of the first-order (direct) consequences. Figure below gives the output of such a process.

Figure 34: Second-Order Consequences

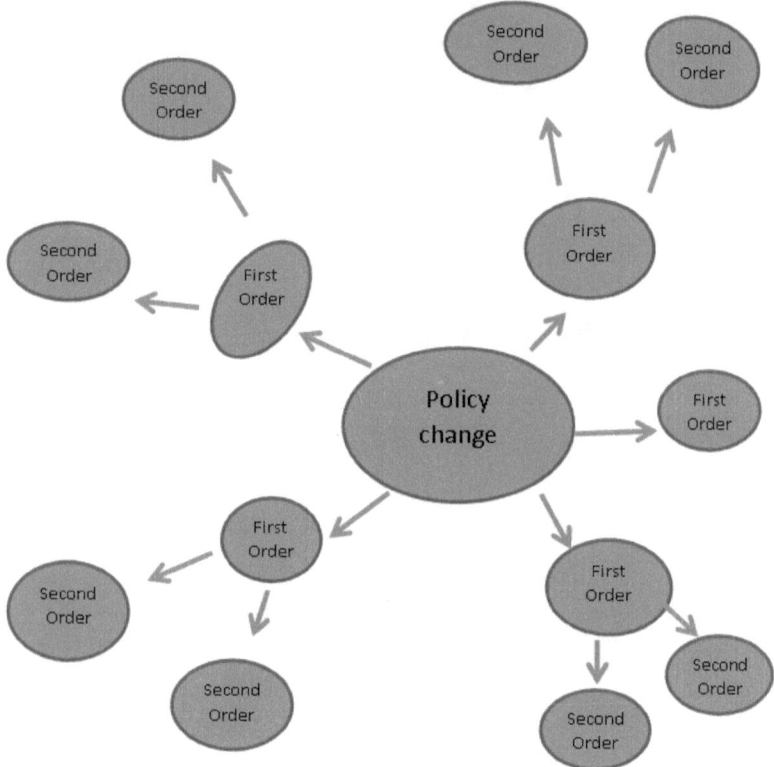

- We can repeat this by identifying the third-order consequences, fourth-order consequences and so on until we can see all plausible consequences.

- That is, after identifying the consequences, go to their logical end. Indeed, when you complete all the levels, you will have a picture of the possible direct and indirect consequences resulting from the policy change. When you list possible consequences, then do an evidence based evaluation and drop out those that don't make sense in the light of the policy change in place.

Figure 35: Third-Order Consequences

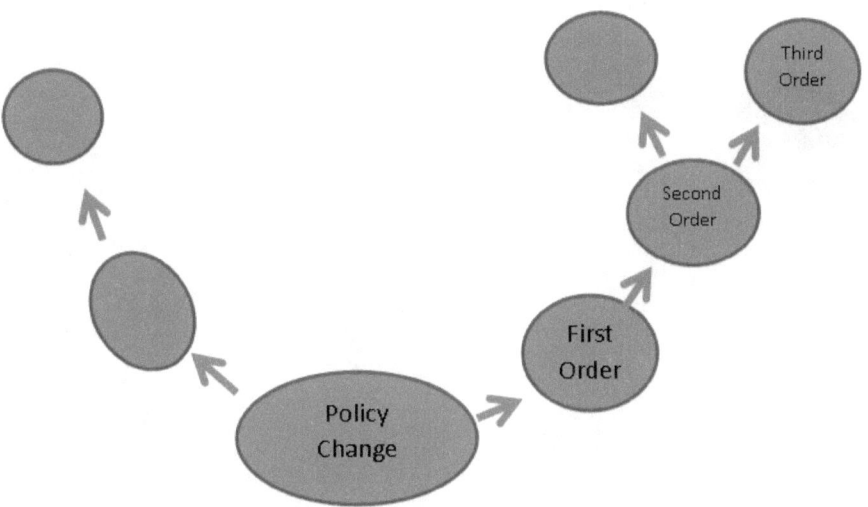

Working with the future-wheel, students analyzed the policy change of a rise in petroleum costs in Zimbabwe. A variety of first-, second-, and third-order consequences came out.

Figure 36: Rise in Petroleum Costs

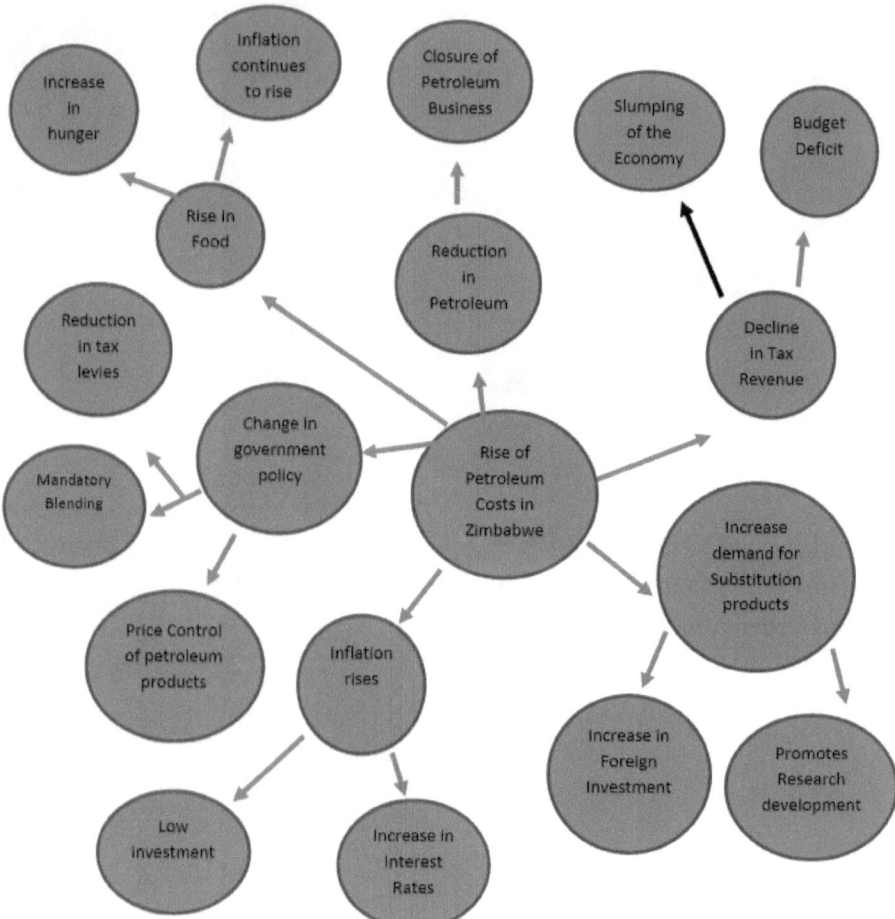

8.2 The Future Wheel on Increasing Oil Prices

In Zambia a class played with the futures wheel on increased oil prices:

Figure 37: Increased Oil Prices

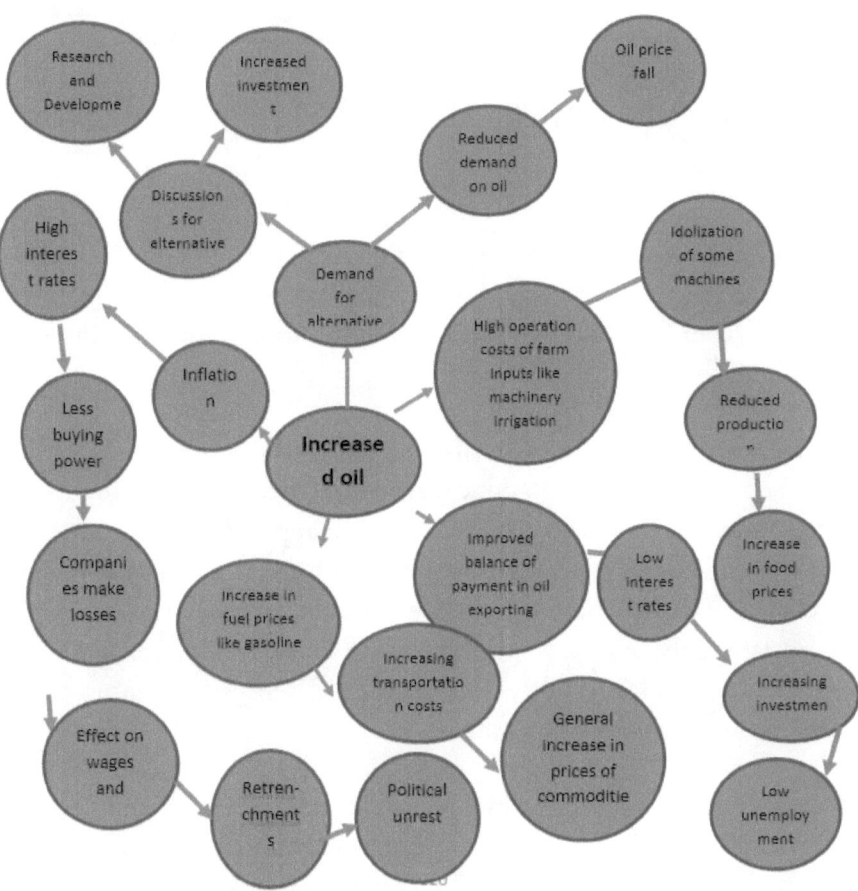

In both these exercises for analytical purposes, the cause-effect analysis can be narrowed down to some major consequences such as the political, economic, administration, technology, social, legal, and financial consequences as illustrated in the student exercises. Real policy implications can then be drawn out of such consequence analysis.

CHAPTER 9

Field Anomaly Relaxation Method

A need for some way of projecting alternative futures became clear in the 1960s when the Douglas Aircraft Company was trying to develop ten-year corporate plans for its four divisions that built various types of military and civil aircraft.

The idea at the beginning was that the plans from the various divisions could be added together to produce an overall corporate plan. Doubts were raised, however, about this apparently logical approach, as it became clear that the worldviews of the division planners were different. The planners for civil aircraft had assumed a peaceful world with a buyer's market for skilled labor; the military side expected a conflict-ridden world with a scarcity of skilled labor. There were similar differences concerning most of the other assumptions being made.

What was noted was that those views did not deal with the details of a particular aircraft but with the socioeconomic domain in, which the aircraft planners had to work. The two emerging worldviews were not compatible, and the plans were not additive. This finding, that a planner's worldview tends to dominate his or her assumptions and judgments, seems to be even today of near-universal applicability.

The possibility that worldviews might be implicitly flawed led to the development of Field Anomaly Relaxation Method or FAR (Rhyne 1981,

1995A). Rhyne applied FAR to a wide range of social fields in, which business and governmental policies might have to exist.

9.1 Description of the FAR Method

The starting point of Field Anomaly Relaxation (FAR) is Lewin's social field theory to the effect that we all live within "fields" of interactions with other people and events. FAR exploits this idea to explore the imaginable patterns within social fields eliminating any, which do not satisfy a gestalt or whole-patterns assessment of internal coherence. The remaining, internally consistent patterns are then used as stepping-stones to creating paths into the future. The steps across the stones enable FAR to generate story scenarios, not just end-state pictures.

> The first word in FAR thus means the simplified field or relationships for the societal or business environment in, which policy has to be made. Like all simplifications of reality, it is a model, the intention of which is to give a tool for rational and systematic thought about the future's possibilities.

> Each component of the field must have several conceivable conditions; economic growth may be high, low, or stagnant, and so on, the conditions differing in kind as well as in degree. The idea is to create 'filing space' for all plausible possibilities.[4] For example, one of the possibilities for the political aspect might be "instability."

> FAR aims to provide a backdrop of internally consistent futures as contexts for policy formulation and decision making. The contexts should normally not be tailored to any specific decision; rather, they should be potentially applicable for broader policy-making and decision analysis across the organization as a whole by providing consistent and coherent views of the future. The aim of FAR is to illuminate strategic questions, not to answer them.

---

[4]   https://libarynth.org/future_fabulators/field_anomaly_relaxation

How to Do FAR

It is a four-stage process, as described below:

1. Step 1 requires one to develop some kind of imaginative view of the future into, which the decision must unfold.

2. Step 2 requires one to identify the critical uncertainties and their ranges of possibility, expressed in a matrix.

3. Step 3 eliminates the anomalies.

4. Step 4 strings the surviving configurations together to form time lines.

Figure 38: The FAR Cycle (after Rhyne)

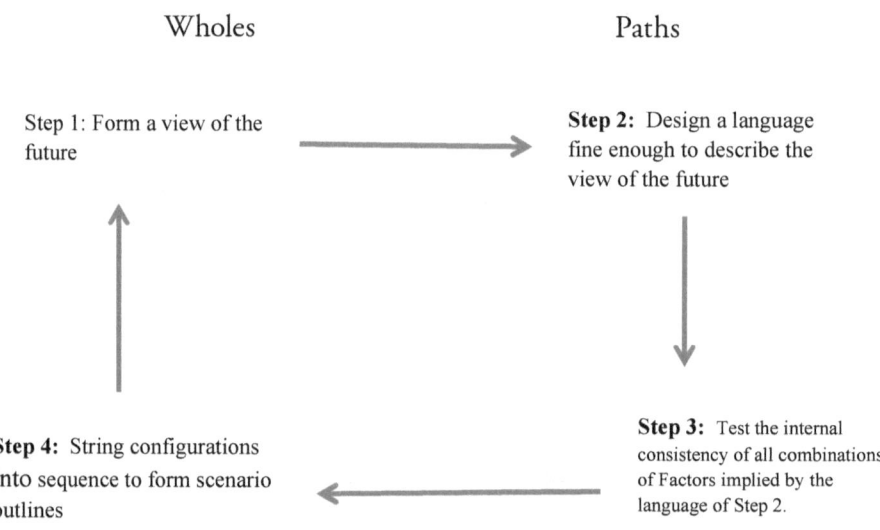

Wholes   Paths

Step 1: Form a view of the future

Step 2: Design a language fine enough to describe the view of the future

Step 4: String configurations into sequence to form scenario outlines

Step 3: Test the internal consistency of all combinations of Factors implied by the language of Step 2.

FAR is cyclic in that the scenarios developed in Step 4, along with appreciations gained, will provide all needed inputs to Step 1 of a subsequent cycle, leading to better scenarios and deeper appreciations. This convergence toward a satisfactory solution is called relaxation in engineering, hence the full name of Field *Anomaly Relaxation.*

In practice, the first cycle may produce such good scenarios that the added effort may not be worthwhile. In any case, decision makers may require the scenarios urgently as a basis for judgment, and time may not be available for a second cycle. Rhyne states that whenever two full-dress FAR cycles have been pursued, one adjustment has been a radical modification of the sector/factor array generated during the first cycle.

Whether there are one or two iterations, the process ends by using the time lines as the plots around, which stories of the future can be written. FAR leads to a collection of short stories rather than one extended narrative. In use by the author, it typically leads to about four scenarios, though Rhyne's work often gave rise to as many as ten.

9.2 Illustration

We now illustrate that FAR process using the South China Sea case study, which sought to develop unofficial scenarios as contexts for policy-making on country X's trade and defense relationships with, and economic support for, other nations in COMESA. A mind map, as in Figure 39, shows the various factors that might play for COMESA integration. These factors range from internal member state configuration to global politics.

Organizing FAR one need to first visualize the Future. This is best done by asking five or six members of the steering group to write short essays in, which they imagine what the future might be, for instance, the East African Community or SADC or COMES. They might be allowed to choose their own themes, or they might be given guidance, such as "Write about a gloomy future." That does not necessarily mean that one aims at a gloomy scenario. The aim is to tease out the factors the essayists see as significant to the region's future. It may turn out that a gloomy scenario will not emerge from the final analysis. The same process works well whether the context is the socioeconomic field for a business firm, the industry in, which it operates, or transport planning for a city. It is, however, vital that the essayists work independently and that they draw on deep knowledge of the problem domain using whatever data and information is available.

Second, write a narrative of that future. It is the end result, somewhat on the lines of an "informed future" (Macrae 1994).

Table 8: ESPARC Sector / Factor Array

E	S	P	A	R	C
Regional Economic Dimension	Regional Political Stability	External Power Dimension	Regional Co-operation Alliance	Regional Resource Pressure	Country's Attitude
E1: Rosy growth	S1: Strong and stable	P1: Effective and very influential	A1: Close co-operation	R1: Low pressure	C1: Leader and policeman
E2: Fair growth	S2: Fairly stable	P2: Fairly influential	A2: Loose multi-literalism	R2: Moderate pressure	C2: One of us
E3: Stifled growth	S3: Shaky	P3: Limited influence	A3: No multi-literalism	R3: High pressure	C3: Minds own business
E4: Negative growth	S4: Unstable		A4: Enmity	R4: Crisis situation	C4: Pushy, verbally
					C5: Forceful, military
					C6: Warlike

Adapted and modified from Tom Ritchey, *Modeling Alternative Futures* (2011)

9.3 Discussion of the Factors

The sequences of the factors in the columns of Table 9 are chosen simply for convenience. In the Economic Dimension column, for instance, the progression from E1, Rosy growth, to E4, Negative growth, has no greater significance than that it may make for easy reading of the filing space of possibilities for the economic aspect of the problem.

Further, and this is the vital point, the arrangement in the columns does not mean that a factor can only change to the next adjacent state. Again using E as the example, if the current condition is E2, Fair growth, then, if things get better, the only possible move is to E1, but if they get worse, the move could be to either E2 or E3. Similarly, if the country's attitude now is C3, then it could change to C1, C5, or C6 and does not have to move via C2 or C4. In short, the identifying numbers on the factors are no more important than the labels of files in a filing cabinet. Reading one file in a cabinet does not force one to read only the adjacent file. In FAR, the numbers are only labels and have no other significance.

The clusters are not themselves scenarios but are the bricks from, which scenarios are constructed by an identifying letter and a few words, which characterize that cluster.

9.4 Forming a Sector/Factor Array

Form a sector/factor array in the usual fashion with as much documentation as time permits but, at the very least, explanations of what the sectors (columns) mean.

1. The policy analyst must find a consistent configuration representing the current situation. (In any FAR, simplified or full-scale, if none of the configurations represents the present, there is a *fundamental* flow in the sector/factor array).

2. Write a short description, in five or ten words, of what that condition represents.

3. Record it on a yellow sticker and place it the foot of a whiteboard or flip chart.

4. Find at least two consistent configurations, which are believable, in the gestalt sense, as conditions for the end of the time horizon being used.

5. Write short descriptions on yellow stickers and put them on the board. Space them apart across the board from "worst" to "best"; the yellow stickers should clearly state why they are bad, good, or in-between. In-between does not necessarily mean halfway between good and bad. It might, for instance, mean "pretty good" or "rather worrying."

6. If time allows, find a few more consistent, believable configurations as end points on the time scale, and perhaps for some intermediate states, and record them as before.

7. It should now be easy to connect these six to eight stickers into credible time lines. If not, revisit steps 3 and 4.

9.5 Creating Normative Scenarios

The customary basis of scenario work is to appraise the future's possibilities, the conclusion being, in effect, "Here is what might plausibly happen. Policymakers would be prudent to be aware of these possibilities. Therefore, we should make sure that our policy recommendations are robust against them."

CHAPTER 10

Choosing Policy Options

10.1 Identifying Policy Alternatives

Once the problem has been designed the Policy Analyst must move and use procedures that help generate a large number of alternatives, which later can be reduced to a manageable size. The challenge is to get the best alternative. The best alternative, following rationality thinking should be the "best" alternative among the pool of alternatives. This involves assessing alternatives and their likely-hood to resolve the problem as identified. This is what is called policy recommendation. It requires the selection of appropriate methods for comparing the alternatives and applying them systematically.

Estimating the expected outcomes, effects and impacts of each policy alternative.

Assessing if the predicted policy outcomes for each alternative meet the desired goals for each alternative.

After this initial filter of alternatives, it is possible that some alternatives will fall out. One needs to then continue to do more in-depth analysis of alternatives that make the first cut. Then compare them by showing the strengths and weaknesses of each of these alternatives.

10.2 Techniques in Comparing Alternatives

There are quite a number of techniques used to compare alternatives. They can be grouped into quantitative or qualitative techniques. A combination would strengthen the analysis. Dunn summarized the broad methods from theoretical modeling to intuition (Dunn 1984).

10.3 Theoretical Modeling

Theoretical models identify important variables and specify the nature of the linkages among them. Then each model is used to predict outcomes when one or more of the variables are changed. Models are built from information, experience, expert advice, etc. Constructing a model helps get to the key elements of the situation and focus on the most important concerns. It identifies the key factors and the relationships among them, which will likely be impacted by any proposed policy alternative. These models may be expressed in words, in physical dimensions, or in numerical form.

One commonly used theoretical model is extrapolations. Extrapolation uses the past to predict the future, assuming there are stable patterns. For example, if the population of an area has been growing at 50 percent every ten years, then a graph showing past growth can be extended into coming years to predict future growth. Extrapolation is useful for conducting a baseline analysis, showing what is expected if the status quo or no action alternative is adopted. It is relatively simple and cheap and can be accurate in many circumstances. Data used can be either raw numbers or a computed rate of change. However, extrapolation requires precisely defined criteria and measures as well as accurate measurement. It is most often used when there are linear patterns in the data. Extrapolation, however, is less useful in the cases of new problems, new issues, or new policy areas, where there is little or no past data.

Another most commonly used form of model is linear regression analysis. The most common type of linear regression is called "ordinary least squares regression." Linear regression uses the values from an existing data set consisting of measurements of the values of two variables, X and Y, to develop a model that is useful for predicting the value of the dependent variable Y for given values of X.[5]

10.4 Cost benefit techniques

Cost-benefit analysis is a technique used to evaluate and distinguish between alternative public policy proposals. An attempt is made to value in monetary terms all the factors involved, be they commercial, social or environmental, regardless of to whom the costs and benefits accrue.

Useful Steps in Analysis of Options

We start with identified policy alternative proposals; then we quantify the gains, benefits, losses, or costs of each alternative. Second, we discount the benefits or costs (putting all costs and benefits on a common temporal footing). Then finally, we work out sets of decision criteria such as net present value, internal rate of return or cost effectiveness or net efficiency ratios. In this approach it is always assumed that the policy alternatives are good if the benefit is found to be higher than costs. Hence the best choice option will be the one that has the highest net efficiency or net effectiveness.

Challenges Working with Cost-Benefit

There are challenges to work with cost-benefit analysis. They range from occasional lack of agreement on appropriate rates like discount rates and reliable monetary equivalents to abuse of data in doing the calculations. These may even arise, for example, in calculating decision criteria such as net present value, internal rate of return, or cost-benefit ratio. Hence, there are controversies in the application of cost-benefit analysis. These include the following:

a)   Which costs and benefits are included?
b)   Can all of these be valued in monetary terms?

---

[5]   https://web.csulb.edu/~msaintg/ppa696/696regs.htm

c) What is the appropriate discount rate? For example, a high discount rate implies a low value on the welfare of future generations.

d) The technique focuses on efficiency and is less helpful with questions of equity.

The existence of these problems with cost-benefit analysis doesn't mean that it shouldn't be applied in decision making. It should, however, influence how much weight we give to the results. Carrying out a cost-benefit analysis will reveal a lot of valuable insights in relation to the policy alternatives before us, even if we are not overly confident of the final quantitative results of the exercise.

10.5 Sensitivity Analysis

In sensitivity analysis, a policy analyst will usually try to see how sensitive the analysis is to changes in assumptions. This involves asking, "What if ... then what?"

This question can be asked regarding all important variables, including the following:

a) the length of the project (how long will benefits continue?)
b) the discount rate
c) the value placed on various quantities (costs, benefits, probabilities, and so on)

10.6 Risk Analysis

The level of risk associated with policy interventions is an important consideration in decision making. Some decision makers are risk averse and may want to minimize any possible losses rather than pursue the (riskier) maximum possible gains.

One way to begin to appreciate the different possible outcomes of different policy alternatives is to use quick decision analysis. This is a way to visually represent a small number of alternatives and their consequences.

Quick decision analysis identifies key issues, and help the policy analyst to decide what information is necessary to assess each possible alternative. It helps structure thinking about the probability or likelihood that certain outcomes will occur. It also helps the policy analysts or decision makers reveal their attitudes about risk and uncertainty. And it alerts the policy analyst to the possible political ramifications of predicted outcomes.

10.6.1 The Process in Risk Analysis

a) Identify the dimensions of the analysis (problem, alternatives, and outcomes).
b) Forecast the likely outcome for each alternative.
c) Assess how likely each outcome is in terms of probability.
d) Calculate the expected value of each alternative.

The process is simple, but the policy analyst must get answers to the following questions:

a) What studies were used to estimate outcomes and probabilities?
b) What discount rate was applied?
c) What time frame was considered?
d) What were the opportunity costs (how could the money be spent elsewhere?)
e) How sensitive are these figures to changes in the economy?
f) At what probability would the expected value of the two alternatives be equal?

After answering these questions, if there is still a great deal of uncertainty about the analysis, we use a number of strategies to improve the analysis, among them:

a) Map out all uncertainties and the information that is needed.
b) Collect more data to reduce uncertainty.
c) Estimate a wide range of possible values for those that are uncertain.

d) Develop alternatives under a wide range of possible conditions.
e) Build in more flexibility.
f) Build in more backup.
g) Compromise to an acceptable alternative, even if it is not the optimal one.
h) Choose a strategy that minimizes the maximum possible losses.
i) Conduct in-depth research to provide the information needed.

It is useful to translate several of these techniques to rank-order the options. The policy analyst must present the benefits and drawbacks of each alternative. But usually there will be many challenges in trying to determine, which policy option to adopt, as many policy problems have multiple facets. There may be no dominant objective, or several objectives may be in conflict.

Hence multiple criteria must be taken into account, including the technical, economic, political, and administrative—but who decides, which is the most important? The choice is the more difficult, as policy choices will deal with future consequences.

The key question is, What change is expected to occur through the policy, and roughly when? Hence each option needs to be assessed in its potential to meet expected outcomes. This requires identifying levels of outcomes whether they are immediate, intermediate, or long term outcomes. Such a process also requires distinguishing policy options from implementation options, putting forward policy options first and then exploring options for implementation of a given policy. (For each policy option identified, there could be several alternative approaches to implement the policy.)

We can also compare several rationalities together using some intuitive models as shown below:

10.7 Comparing Options Using Different Rationalities

A complete option analysis requires taking and comparing the identified options through several rationalities. Table 9 illustrates how to compare/ do a feasibility assessment of options.

Table 9: Different Rationalities Elements

Option	Ec	Fi	Ad	So	Po	Le	Te	Total
A								
B								
C								
D								

- Ec: Economic Rationality

- Fi: Financial Rationality

- Ad: Administrative Rationality

- So: Social Rationality

- Po: Political Rationality

- Le: Legal Rationality

- Te: Technological Rationality

10.7.1 Constraint Mapping

After we identify possible options and we weight them through multiple rationalities, it is important also to do a constraint map for each option.

The constraint map requires identifying or clarifying limitations or obstacles that stand in the way of achieving policy objectives for each possible alternative. These include such constraints as physical, legal, organizational/ political/ distributional, and budgetary constraints.

These constraints may not prevent the policy analyst from picking one option, but it is important for the policy analyst to identify the would-be constraints.

10.7.2 Cost Internalization

For each option we may also have to do cost internalization. Cost Internationalization is a procedure for incorporating all relevant outside costs into the internal cost element structure. For example, costs of pollution, environmental degradation, or social dislocation nowadays must explicitly be included by most analysis and should be built into the process of recommendation.

10.7.3 Conclusion

The risk analysis method of recommendation involves many uncertainties because it is about both facts and values. Therefore, the purpose of policy recommendation is not simply to forecast or predict some future outcome but to advocate a course of action whose consequences are valued and ethical (Dunn 1981). Recommendation will also involve policy argumentation, which is the main vehicle for communicating the results of policy analysis. A policy analyst is unlikely to succeed unless he/she can translate the technical vocabularies into arguments that can be understood by policymakers and stakeholders. "The dynamic process of structuring a decision problem involves specification of options, attributes for evaluating such options and understanding the state of nature that may occur" (Koller and Joanal 1989).

CHAPTER 11

Policy Monitoring and Evaluation

11.1 Policy Monitoring

Policy monitoring is a process of observation and recording of policy activities. Its main purpose is to produce information and feedback about the policy (Burtle 2014).

The BusinessDictionary.com defines monitoring as a process of "supervising activities in progress to ensure they are on-course and on-schedule in meeting the objectives and policy performance targets" (Business Dictionary 2014). Policy monitoring helps the policy analyst and policy actors to watch where the policy is going.

11.2 Purpose of Policy Monitoring

Generally, policy monitoring fulfills three major purposes in the policy process: efficiency, effectiveness, and consent. However, in general terms policy monitoring "helps determine when different policy actions are required and whether the level of policy intervention needs to be changed so that the policy objectives can be achieved" (T.R.C. 1995).

A good policy monitoring framework should be designed such that it can be used to help determine how well the policy is working in practice. Hence it should be designed as part of the policy design phase. The objectivity of the instrument lies in it being designed before we start seeing the implementation results.

11.3 Policy Efficiency Monitoring (PEM)

PEM helps to measure the extent to, which given policy outputs are achieved with minimum waste of resources. With PEM we are looking at costs relative to results. Efficiency is measured by the ratio of benefits to costs. The most efficient policy will be the one that achieves the desired outcomes with the least cost (Willis, 2008).

11.4 Policy Consent Monitoring

In the public sector, an activity that is authorized must be monitored to ensure that the consent holder is complying with the conditions of that consent during the use of the "resource." Compliance involves inspection to ensure the consent holder complied with the consent conditions or permitted activity standards.

11.5 Levels of Policy Monitoring

Policy monitoring will differ depending on the level at, which the monitoring is focusing. If the unit of analysis is the country, we can monitor the policy either at national level, regional level, or district level. For an organization, the focus could be board level, management level, function, etc. Policy monitoring methods will differ at each of these levels. Information generated will also differ according to the specific objectives for monitoring.

11.5.1 National Level

This is the macro level sitting. At this level the policy analyst will be interested, first, in finding out if the policy outputs are effective—that is, whether the overall planned outputs are being realized. The learning is about whether the policy design was appropriate. Secondly, at this level we want to learn whether the policy outcomes are coming as intended. At this level, therefore, the objectives of policy monitoring are to generate data so that the analyst can

- ensure policy inputs are being used effectively and efficiently;

- understand whether the planned policy activities are being implemented;

- determine whether policy inputs are being well utilized;

- find out if the resources are reaching the intended people;

- assess the usefulness and applicability of the methods being used to implement the policy; and

- draw some lessons for future policy design and implementation (P. Bartle 2014; Dunn 1981).

11.5.2 Regional/Provincial Level

In countries where there is a regional or provincial or county administration of policy, the central policy monitoring function is more of a coordinating process. The provincial office gets information from the lower levels. This data from various counties or districts in the province or region is aggregated to monitor the effect of national policy across the country.

11.5.3 Sub-District Level

Eventually policy impact will be felt at the household level. At this level is where policy success or failure takes place. Therefore, the major purpose of policy monitoring at this level is foremost to improve the implementability of the policy. In more specific terms we need to collect data so that we can

- ensure policy inputs are utilized efficiently to create value for money;

- ensure the policy is being implemented as scheduled; and

- ensure the policy implementation is of good quality and leading to planned policy goals.

11.6 Monitoring Indicators

To be able to understand what is going on, it is important from the outset of policy design to agree on the monitoring indicators. Monitoring indicators can be qualitative or quantitative criteria for measuring or assessing the achievement of the policy activities and policy objectives. Good monitoring indicators show the extent to, which the policy is being achieved.

Using the systems logic methodologies, there are four commonly used types of monitoring indicators, namely; input, output, outcome, and impact indicators

11.6.1 Policy Input Indicators

The input indicators will describe what resources are going into the policy activities; the input base includes both human and non-human inputs. Time is one major input resource we should not forget to plan for in any monitoring system.

11.6.2 Policy Output Indicators

Policy output indicators describe policy activities and what comes out of them. Outputs come from the policy black box. The outputs are not necessarily equal to the inputs. In the policy black box, the mixing is a creative process.

11.6.3 Policy Outcome Indicators

These indicators describe the product of the policy outputs.

11.6.4 Policy Impact Indicators

These indicators measure the change in the conditions—that is, the difference policy outcomes make on the conditions.

11.7 Policy Evaluation

Policy Logic Framework

To do a good policy evaluation, we need to understand the initial policy logic framework. The logic of a policy is the description of the policy at the four levels of the hierarchy of policy objectives, namely:

- policy inputs

- policy outputs

- policy outcomes

- policy impacts

Defining policy logic helps the analyst to do a complete policy evaluation.

Figure 39: Policy Inputs to Policy Outcomes

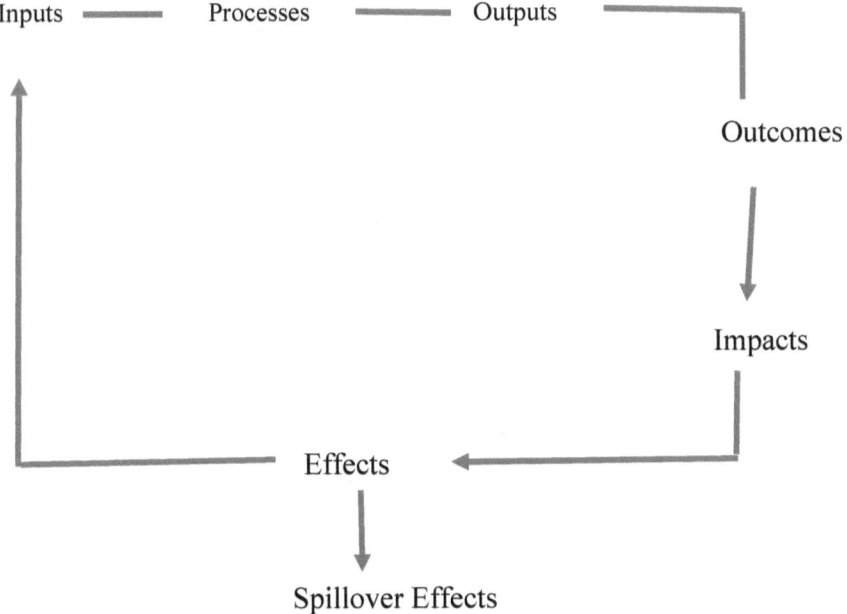

Porteous et al. (2002) and Weiss (1998) argue that the logic model shows the intermediate effects that provide indications of effectiveness. Measuring effectiveness can help confirm that something happened.

The narrative description of the policy intervention logic at each of the four levels gives us a complete picture of the policy narrative.

Figure 40: The Policy Logic

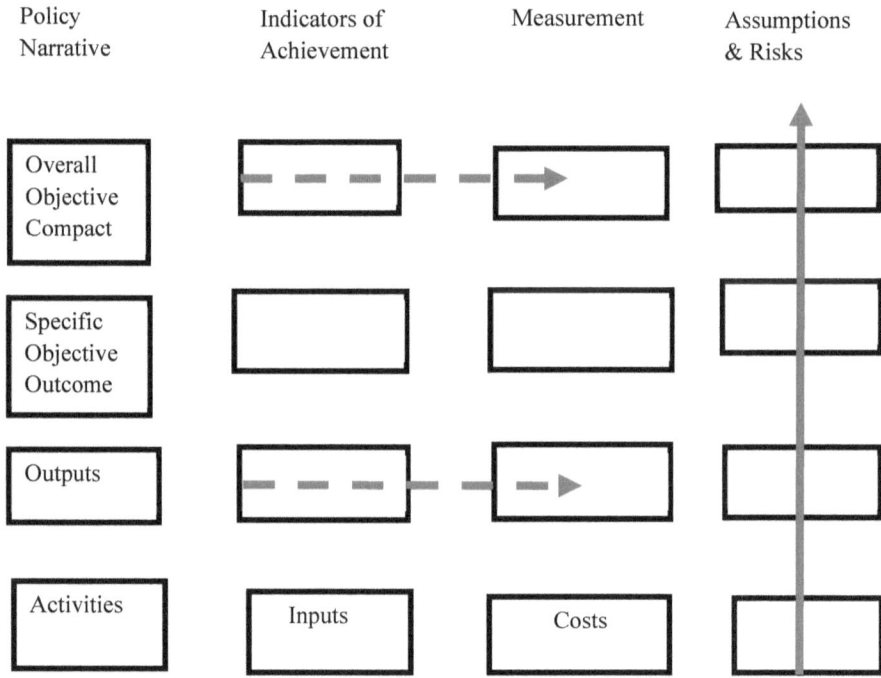

Adopted from Tempus, *Handbook*, 1933

The policy logic results in a chain of inputs, processes, outputs, and impacts. Diagram below illustrates a number of items at each chain level.

Figure 41: Linking Monitoring and Evaluation of Policy Outcomes

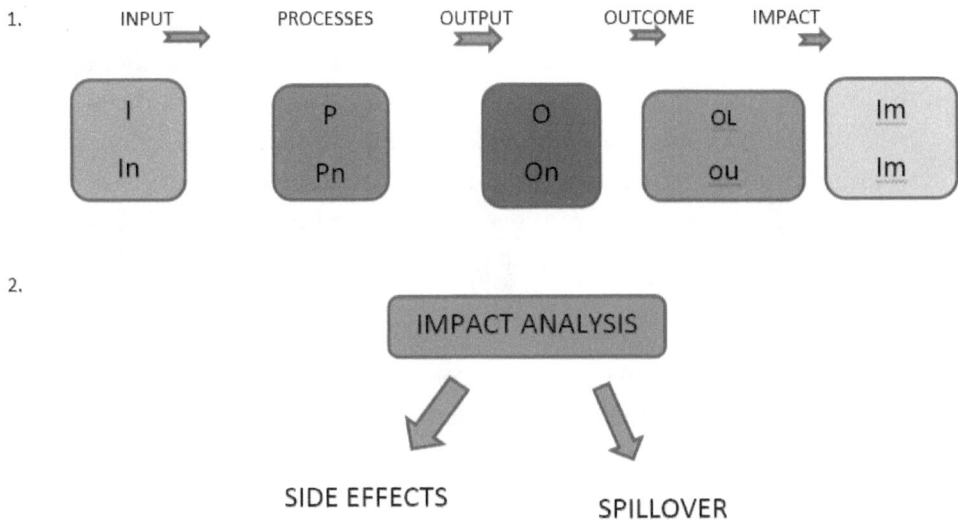

With a policy logic framework, we integrate prospective to retrospective policy analysis and management. A policy logic model can therefore be defined as "the chain of expected effects that link a policy to a problem it aims to solve" (NCC 2013).

It goes beyond the monitoring question, "Does it work?" To gain a better understanding of how it works, that is how the policy at hand is meant to operate. We see the mechanisms of change are not the intervention per se, but the response that the intervention generates (Weiss 1998, 57).

Illustration 1

Figure 42: Policy Logic Model Illustration

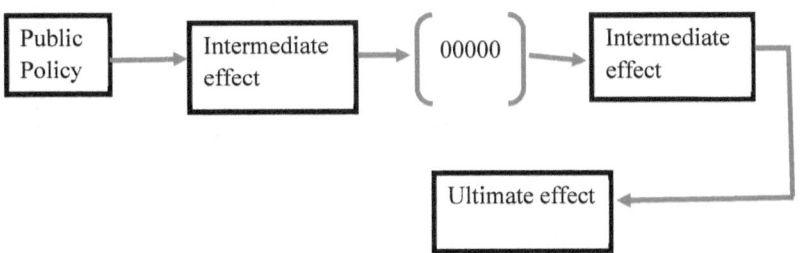

11.8 Constructing a Policy Logic Model

In policy analysis, usually developing a cause-effect relationship between the policy and its effects is problematic (Whitehead 2011), especially where the impacts take effect or come into view after a long time. On the other hand, even if the effects are immediate, these effects may be influenced by other ex-policy factors—external factors to the policy—such that the policy is only one such factor influencing the targeted problem (Milton et al. 2011). So designing the policy logic model can help us reduce the risk of passing judgment on policy without controlling for extraneous factors.

A well-designed policy logic model "can provide feedback to the effectiveness of the policy being evaluated while strengthening the presumption of a causal connection" (Weiss 1998).

Steps in Constructing the Logic Model

First: Start with the policy as an independent variable (X), and work out the desired impact (dependent variable Y).

Second: Develop the logic (cause-effect) x Y ⟶

                                    Policy Effects.

Third: In reality the policy would have several ultimate effects.

Fourth: Develop logical steps that will occur if we were to move from X to Y.

Fifth: Use the logic of "if/then" to create a number of statements showing the direction of the effects of the policy.

Sixth: A policy value chain can be developed sometime with periodization of effects.

The easiest way to construct a policy model is to make it linear. Then of course a number of paths and effects can be increased and then made complex by introducing external factors: contingencies, spillover effects, side effects, etc. (Mayne 2008; De-Vlaming 2010).

The policy logic narrative creates the pathway to use for evaluating the impact of the policy. It also helps from the policy design stage to see the logic of the policy being designed and whether the expected outcomes are the right ones. Defining policy logic is also important in that it helps in choosing the right policy options.

Hence a good policy logic framework links monitoring information to policy evaluation. "If we can show that a policy works up to a certain point in the chain of effects, we can get a better idea of its contribution to the ultimate effect" (Weiss 1998; Mayne 2008).

In this policy value chain, policy evaluation is an objective process of understanding how a policy or other intervention was implemented, what effects it had, for whom, how, and why. To be useful, policy evaluations need to be tailored to the type of policy being considered, and the types of questions it is expected to answer.

Therefore, the earlier an evaluation is considered in the policy development cycle, the more likely it will be that the most appropriate type of evaluation can be identified and adopted. Good-quality policy evaluations should generate reliable results, which can be used and disseminated with confidence. Policy evaluation as feedback mechanism can enable policies to be improved or can justify reinvestment or resource savings, as policy evaluation can show whether or not policies are delivering as planned and resources are being effectively used.

Good-quality policy evaluations will play an important role in setting and delivering on priorities and objectives, demonstrating accountability, and providing defensible evidence to independent scrutiny processes where required. Policy evaluation also contributes valuable knowledge to the policy evidence base, which can be fed into future policy development.

Danger!

- Not evaluating, or evaluating poorly, will mean that policymakers will not be able to provide meaningful evidence in support of any claims they might wish to make about a policy's effectiveness.

Policy Evaluation Process

There are several ways that evaluation fits into the policy cycle, as shown in the diagram below. In general terms, policy evaluation helps create learning on what works and what does not. With policy evaluation we assume policy adoption has taken place.

Figure 43: Policy Analysis Framework

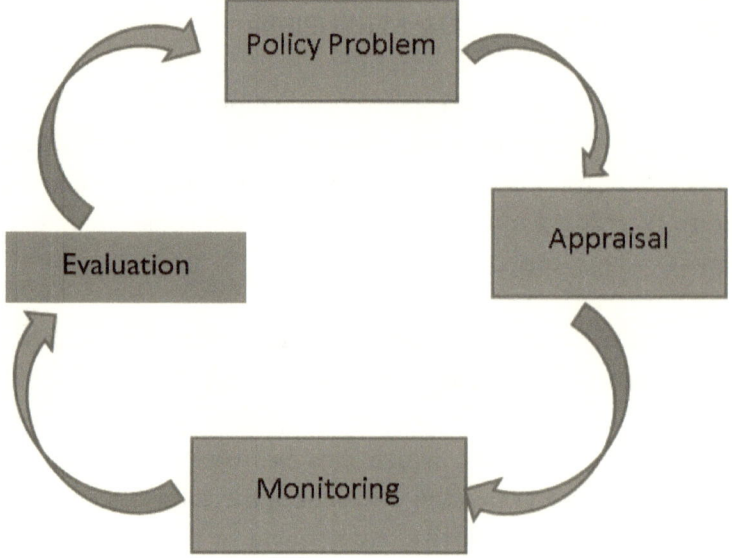

Evaluation

- Appraisal occurs after the rationale and objectives of the policy have been formulated. The purpose is to identify the best way of delivering on the policy prior to implementation. It involves identifying a list of options that meet the stated objectives and assessing them for the costs and benefits that they are likely to bring.

- Monitoring seeks to check progress against planned targets and can be defined as the formal reporting and evidencing that outputs are successfully delivered and milestones met.

- Evaluation is the assessment of the policy effectiveness and efficiency during and after implementation. It seeks to measure outcomes and impacts in order to assess whether the anticipated benefits have been realized.

11.9 Identifying the Right Evaluation for the Policy

- It is important to identify the right way to evaluate the policy. There are usually three broad classes of questions, which evaluation might be used to answer:

  o How was the policy delivered?

  o What differences did the policy make?

  o Did the benefits of the policy justify the costs?

11.10 How Was the Policy Delivered? Process Evaluation

The question of how the policy was delivered is concerned with the processes associated with the policy, the activities involved in its implementation, and the pathways by, which the policy was delivered.

These processes vary quite considerably according to the nature of the policy in question; therefore, there is no simple, generic characterization of questions such as those that tend to be applicable when, for example, doing impact evaluation.

In general, process-related questions are intentionally descriptive. As a result, process evaluations can employ a wide range of data collection and analysis techniques, covering multiple topics and participants, tailored to the processes specific to the policy in question.

These wide ranges of data will often include the collection of qualitative and quantitative data from different stakeholders using, for example, group interviews or one-to-one interviews and surveys. These surveys might cover subjective issues (such as perceptions of how well a policy has operated) or objective aspects (perhaps the factual details of how a policy has operated).

They might also be used to collect organizational information (for instance, how much time was spent on particular activities), although an administrative source (timesheets and personnel data, for instance) might be more reliable, if available.

Although essentially descriptive, these types of information can be vital to measuring the inputs of an intervention (which might not be limited to simple financial budgets but might also include staff and other resources "levered in" from elsewhere) as well as the outcomes (surveys might be used to measure aspects of a scheme's participants' quality of life, for instance).

11.11 What Difference Did the Policy Make? Outcome Evaluation

The question of what difference a policy has made involves a focus on the outcomes of the policy. Outcomes are those measurable achievements that either are themselves the objectives of the policy or at least contribute to them, as well as the benefits they generate.

11.12 Key Questions to Be Asked Focus on Outcomes

For example, what were the policy outcomes, were there any observed changes, and if so, how much change was there from what was already in place? And how much could be said to have been caused by the policy as opposed to other factors? Did the policy achieve its stated objectives?

How did any change vary across different individuals, stakeholders, sections of society, and so on, and how did they compare with what was expected?

Did outcomes occur that were not originally intended, and if so, what and how significant were they?

These questions relating to what difference the policy made concern the change in outcomes caused by the policy, or the policy "impact"; hence the term *impact evaluation*. The key characteristic of a good impact evaluation is that it recognizes that most outcomes are affected by a range of factors, not just the policy. To test the extent to, which the policy was responsible for the change, it is necessary to estimate (usually on the basis of often quite technical statistical analysis of quantitative data) what would have happened in the absence of the policy. This is known as the counterfactual.

Establishing the counterfactual is not easy, since by definition it cannot be observed. It is what would have happened if the policy had not gone ahead. A good evaluation therefore is one that successfully isolates the effect of the policy from all other potential influences, thereby producing a good estimate of the counterfactual.

11.13 Did the Benefits Justify the Costs? Economic Evaluation

A reliable impact evaluation might be able to demonstrate and quantify the outcomes generated by a policy but will not on its own be able to show whether those outcomes justified the policy. Economic evaluation is able to consider such issues, including whether the costs of the policy have been outweighed by the benefits.

11.14 Types of Economic Evaluation

Cost-effectiveness analysis (CEA) values the costs of implementing and delivering the policy and relates this amount to the total quantity of outcome generated, to produce a "cost per unit of outcome" estimate (e.g., cost per additional individual placed in employment);

Cost-benefit analysis (CBA) goes further than CEA in placing a monetary value on change outcomes as well (e.g., the value of placing an additional individual in employment). This means that CBA can examine the overall justification of a policy ("Do the benefits outweigh the costs?").

11.15 What Type of Evaluation for the Policy?

The answers from process evaluations are more descriptive, while the answers from impact evaluations as more definitive and in some sense robust. This is because good impact evaluations attempt to control for all other factors that could generate an observed outcome. That is, they attempt to estimate the counterfactual.

11.16 Building Impact Evaluation into Policy Design

Key Points

Impact evaluations have special requirements and benefits for being considered during the policy design stage, because of the need to understand what would have occurred in the absence of the policy.

One of the keys to good evaluation is obtaining a reliable estimate of the counterfactual. This is frequently a significantly challenging part of policy evaluation, because of the often very large number of factors, other than a policy itself, that drive the kinds of outcome measures relevant to public policy. But a good policy must have a positive impact.

CHAPTER 12

Writing Policy Papers

The purpose of the policy paper is to provide a comprehensive and persuasive argument justifying the policy recommendations presented in the paper and therefore to act as a decision making tool and a call to action for the target audience.

12.1 Designing Solutions for Real-World Problems

Unlike traditional academia, which focuses on building knowledge within a group of peers, a policy paper must address real-world problems and therefore provide recommendations and a framework for their application within the targeted society.

For example, it is not enough to analyze the causes and patterns of unemployment in a particular society in order to contribute to its understanding as a social phenomenon.

A policy study must apply this knowledge to the real situation on the ground by understanding the causes, showing that it is a problem within the community in question, and suggesting a course of action to address the problem. Hence, the problem-solution relationship must be seen at the heart of the discipline, which means that any analysis undertaken must be driven and targeted on the search for a practical, implementable, and comprehensive outcome.

The search for such a practical outcome not only requires a well-elaborated and comprehensive analysis of all available data, but as the issues under consideration are of a societal nature, the policy researcher or analyst will also have to make some value-driven judgments about the outcome that would best address the specific problem. Hence, proposing specific solutions in the highly politicized environment of public policy and to such a broad audience means that central to the work of the policy specialist is not just the cold empiricism of data analysis; probably even more important is the ability to convince your audience of the suitability of your policy recommendations.

In other words, the presentation of the outcomes of your data analysis will probably not be enough to make an impact in the policy debate on a particular issue, but through the use of this data as evidence in a comprehensive and coherent argument of your position, you will give your work the best possible chance of having this impact. Majone (1989) sums up this idea excellently:

> Like surgery, the making of policy and the giving of policy advice are exercises of skills, and we do not judge skillful performance by the amount of information stored in the head of the performer or by the amount of formal planning. Rather, we judge it by criteria like good timing and attention to details; by the capacity to recognize the limits of the possible, to use limitations creatively, and to learn from one's mistakes; by the ability not to show what should be done, but to persuade people to do what they know should be done.

12.2 Policy Paper Planning Checklist

In preparing to write your policy paper, consider the policy making process that you are involved in and research that you (and your colleagues) have done (Eylin and Quinn 2002).

Key preliminary questions need to be answered, namely:

- Which stage(s) in the policy making process are you trying to influence through your policy paper?

- Which stakeholders have been/are involved at each stage of the policy making process?

- Have you identified a clear problem to address? Can you summarize it in two sentences?

- Do you have sufficiently comprehensive evidence to support your claim that a problem exists?

- Have you outlined and evaluated the possible policy options that could solve this problem? What evaluation criteria did you use?

- Have you decided on a preferred alternative?

- Do you have sufficient evidence to effectively argue for your chosen policy alternative over the others?

12.3 Sample Formats

Guidelines to Understanding How Major Government Policy Papers Are Written

Many governments have a common format for presenting government policy papers. These are called policy documents or cabinet memoranda.

Guidelines to Policy Documents and Cabinet Memoranda

A policy refers to a statement of goals, objectives, targets, and courses of action. This will have the following sections:

- government vision

- rationale

- objectives

- a set of concerns

- a set of actions

This list forms the standard format for preparation of cabinet memoranda

(Kenya 2004). In some governments, adjustments as to the content can be introduced.

As a policy analyst it is important to know that cabinet memoranda are documents used by ministers to seek approval of cabinet on a course of action or inform cabinet on action taken or intended to be taken to deal with an issue. This is a practice in most African countries.

The three types of memorandum commonly used in many African countries are called:

1. agenda memoranda (documents used to seek cabinet approval for a recommendation or a set of recommendations not to do with legislation);

2. information memoranda (documents used to inform cabinet on the decision(s) taken by the minister); and

3. legislative memoranda (agenda memoranda used to seek cabinet approval to introduce new legislation or to amend or repeal existing legislation).

12.4 Guidelines for Best Practices for Writing Policy Documents

These guidelines help ministers comply with cabinet decisions on how to formulate policies to guide their operations or help secure consistency in the presentation of policy documents to cabinet.

The key elements of the format are as follows:

Executive Summary

- heading and title of the policy (problem)

- description of the subject matter of policy

- sector-based, not necessarily synonymous with the portfolio.

- foreword

- description of the expected results

- challenges

- signature of the minister or chief policymaker

Technique

The executive summary should be clear and focused. It should never refer to the body of the paper. The busy policymaker after reading the executive summary should be able to make sense of what the paper is all about.

Acknowledgement

The initiating ministry should

- acknowledge the effort of all stakeholders who were engaged during the preparation of the policy;

- refer to the means used to develop the policy; and

- ensure the permanent or principal secretary signs this section.

Working Definitions

- define new terms repeatedly used

- define the context in, which they are applied

Acronyms

- list and explain all the abbreviations and symbols

- explain what they stand for

12.5 Structure and Organization of the Document

Introduction

- introduce the subject matter

- explain how it has risen

Situational Analysis

- provides critical review of the existing situation:

  – the background of the policy problem

  – the causes

  – the current status

The Vision

- states what the situation would be at a set time after the policy has been implemented

- sets the targets for the future

Guiding Principle

- underlying principles on which the policy is founded

- fundamental values of the country upon which policy is based

Objectives

- define what the policy intends to achieve in future. This statement needs to be SMART (specific, measurable, achievable, realistic, and time-specific)

Measures

- attain the set objectives and also define the roles, responsibilities, and functions of various stakeholders involved or proposed

Implementation Framework

Under this section the policy analyst need to:

a) Specify institutional arrangements required to implement the proposed policy,

b) Specify any legal framework,(Identify laws), which may impede or facilitate successful implementation of the policy.

c) Resource mobilization— Define or /outline the resources that will be required to implement the proposed policy. Also identify the potential sources and how such resources can be mobilized. For example, will the resources be internally mobilized or based on grants or loans? From local or international borrowing? If borrowing identify the impact of such on the macro economics of the country.

d) Monitoring and evaluation—Identify and outline mechanisms and institutions to be used in monitoring and evaluation of the proposed policy impacts.

12.6 Guidelines for Writing an Agenda Memorandum

In the sections above, we have presented a general format. However, depending on the type of memorandum, the emphasis changes in some subtitles. Let us examine each type of the memorandum, in detail.

Heading and Title

This is designed to identify the principal subject to be discussed and resolved. Therefore, this is shown on the cover page and first page of the main body. The heading in many countries is drawn from approved cabinet standard subject headings.

The heading should be followed by the title, which best summarizes the issue to be resolved. The title should be short. The best practice is for the title not to exceed ten words. It means it has to be simple and clear. Then below the heading and title write the following: "Memorandum by the Minister/Secretary of …."

Minister's Recommendation(s)

This is the proposed course(s) of action for, which the minister is seeking cabinet approval. It must be concise, comprehensive, and factual. Always never refer the reader to the main text). You should note or remember that the minister's recommendation must be clear, precise and logical. It should specify all required actions. If the announcement will be through a press release, you need to attach it. The press release must show timing and method of announcement.

Summary of Issues to Be Resolved

This section provides a sentence summary of the subject to be discussed and issues to be resolved by cabinet. It links title to recommendation(s).

Rationale

It provides justification for the memorandum by explaining the following: first, relationship between proposed and existing government policy; second, argument in support of memorandum; third, consequence of not accepting the recommendation; fourth, detail of specific proposal and how outcomes are to be achieved.

Background

This section outlines the background to the proposal, which outlines the following:

- how the issue arose

- the major developments that led the minister to bring the issue to cabinet

- whether to refer to earlier papers and records of decision taken by cabinet contingent on if or where the issue has already been considered by cabinet

Resource Requirement

Outlines full range of resources required including financial and non-financial resources and the period when they are required.

Doing resource analysis, the following need to be taken into account; namely:

1. whether agreed with the treasury

2. any factors that may affect accuracy of the estimates

3. sources of funding

4. time frame for resources

Impact

Indicate the likely positive and negative impacts of the proposal. Show also other options that were considered and the cost-benefit analysis of each option done before taking the choice being proposed.

Implementation Plan

An implementation plan as part of the proposal must show

- direction for implementing the proposal;

- who does what, when, which indicators to assess achievement;

- activities to be carried out;

- the implementing institution;

- time frames, if any;

- the arrangement for monitoring and evaluation system; and

- urgency, immediacy, and timing.

Summary Elements in an Agenda Memorandum

A Cover Page of a policy must show a good presentation of a Summary of the recommendations. The summary has the following sub titles:

i. issues to be resolved by the proposed policy,

ii. rationale of the proposed policy,

iii. background of the proposed policy,

iv. resources required to effectively implement the proposed policy,

v. impact of proposed policy,

vi. other options considered,

vii. consultations done with key stakeholders,

viii. implementation plan of the proposed policy,

ix. urgency, immediacy, and timing of the proposed policy

The summary is written in the sequence i to ix.

12.7 Guidelines for Writing Legislation Memorandum

- A legislation memorandum is also an agenda memorandum. However, where a desired outcome cannot be achieved through administrative means, this is a proposal to introduce new legislation or else to amend or repeal existing legislation.

- The steps in drafting a legislation memorandum are as follows:

Step 1

You need approval of memorandum by cabinet in principle then you "write to attorney general's chambers through legal affairs seeking legal opinion as to whether such legislation is required" (this is the practice in most Africa Commonwealth countries).

Step 2

Once the attorney general's chambers and the permanent secretary for legal affairs have agreed to the proposed policy, the relevant ministry then prepares and submits a cabinet memorandum outlining the object of a proposed bill. Then the relevant ministry seeks approval of policy paper (cabinet to introduce legislation in parliament) for approval by legislative committee.

Step 3

When approved by cabinet, the relevant ministry sends drafting instruction to the attorney chambers office. After drafting, then the initiating ministry works on the legislative committee's memorandum, with the aim of securing approval by cabinet for publication and introduction in parliament.

Step 4

When legislation committee has approved the proposed bill, a cabinet memorandum seeking approval for publication and introduction of the bill in parliament is prepared by the initiating ministry and submitted back to cabinet secretariat.

Format for Legislation Memorandum

•   Heading and Title

As with any memorandum we start with a good and specific heading with a title.

The heading for this entire memorandum is "Legislation," while the title is the name of the proposed bill. Then below the heading and title you insert the Minister who is initiating the bill: "Memorandum by the Minister of …."

If it is a joint memorandum the first listed is the main minister.

•   Minister's Recommendation

The recommendation is seeking cabinet approval in principle to the introduction of a bill in parliament to amend legislation. It reads as follows:

"I recommend to cabinet that approval be given in principle to the introduction of a bill in parliament to amend [give the title of the legislation to be amended] to provide that [state what the amended legislation is intended to achieve]."

The recommendation seeking cabinet approval in principle to the introduction of a bill in parliament to repeal reads, "I recommend to cabinet that approval be given to repeal [give the title of legislation to be repealed]in order to [state the reasons for repealing]."

After the minister's recommendations you should come up with the background to proposed course of action identified, defined, and fully discussed.

After the background, outline the following:

- detail of proposed legislation

- how it will lead to desired outcome

- why the issue has arisen

- review of the major developments that led to initiating issue to cabinet

Impact

Outline the likely positive and negative consequences of the change by

- highlighting possible impact on other legislations;

- showing the implementation plan including when you intend to present to parliament; and

- including any consultation done with all stakeholders and copies sent to all members of cabinet.

Urgency, Immediate Action and Timing

- how quickly decision(s) must be conveyed and communicated

- if public statement, attach such draft statement

Request that recommendation be accepted by cabinet

- should request cabinet whether the recommendation in paragraph 1 is accepted

- ends with minister's initial and reference number of the ministerial subject files

Preparation of Draft Legislation

When approval in principle is granted by the cabinet, the original ministry then sends detailed drafting instruction to the attorney general. Such instruction must have the objectives, which the proposed new, repeal, or amendment of legislation intends to achieve.

When the first draft bill is prepared and verified, then it goes back to cabinet.

When the first draft is approved in principle by cabinet, typescript copies of final draft are made, and the chief parliament counsel certifies them before sending them before the ministry.

Confirmation of Draft Bill

Ministry prepares legislation committee memorandum, which, once approved by minister, is then submitted to cabinet office on ministry action file for issue. Should read as follows: "I recommend to the committee that a bill entitled ..., which was approved by cabinet in principle for introduction in parliament and a certified draft copy of which is annexed to the memorandum, be approved for publication." This memorandum should make reference to the original cabinet memorandum in, which cabinet approval of bill in principle was sought as well as the decision of cabinet.

When the draft bill is approved by legislation committee, cabinet secretariat requests ministry to prepare memorandum and present bill in final draft to cabinet for consideration and approval for publication and introduction in parliament. If draft bill is not approved in committee, the chief parliamentary counsel conveys decision to the ministry.

12.7 Guidelines for Writing Information Memorandum

The main sections are similar to any cabinet memorandum, except emphasis changes under the "Minister's Action" stage.

Heading and Title

- shown on cover page and first page of main body

- heading selected from list of approved cabinet standard subject heading

- heading designed to identify the principal subject to be discussed and resolved

- heading followed by title

- title summarizes the issue

- below Heading and Title write, "Memorandum by Minister of ..."

- for joint memorandum, list the main initiating minister and then others

- outline actions minister has/have taken

- outline action(s) minister intends to take

- specify the outcome of action

In the Background

- provide background to the proposed course of action

- how the issue arose

- the major developments that led the initiating minister to take such action

Where item already considered by cabinet, show papers/records.

The purpose of the action taken/ intended:

- Rationale of the policy,

- Show justification and supporting argument the proposed policy,

- why the issue has risen

- the relation of action to existing policy

- the consequences if any if the current situation was to continue or not changed by a new policy,

  - indicate the resources required to effectively implement the proposed policy,

  - likely impact, both positive and negative, of the proposed policy,

The rationale ends with the statement that the minister requests that cabinet take note of information at paragraph 1 (minister's actions). Then the memorandum ends with initials of ministers and reference number of the ministerial subject file.

12.8 Writing a Policy Brief

Unlike Cabinet papers, policy briefs end with someone you are advising. However, the logic is the same: be precise, succinct, and clear as to what your advice is about.

1. Executive summary: This should be a short summary of the purpose of the brief and its recommendations. It typically appears single-spaced on the cover of a brief or position paper. Be as specific as possible. Remember, you need to "speak truth to power."

2. Statement of the Issue/problem: Phrase the topic as a question that requires a decision. This can be as short as one question.

Good questions with, which to start:

- What ... ?

- Should ... ?

- How should ... ?

- Who should ... ?

- When should ... ?

3. Background (of the problem): Include only the essential facts that a decision maker needs to know to understand the context of the problem. Assume that you have been hired to filter through reams of information on behalf of a very busy and sleep-deprived person. Be clear, precise, and succinct.

4. Statement of your brief: This is meant to remind the reader of why the issue matters for the country/group/organization that you are advising.

5. Preexisting policies: This summarizes what has been done (by others and the entity that you represent) about the problem thus far. The objective of this section is to inform the reader of policy options that have already been pursued, if any. Note that the absence of action may be considered a policy decision (Dye 1972).

6. Policy options: This delineates the possible courses of action or inaction that your organization may pursue. Please provide the decision maker with *at least three potential courses of action.* Some of them may be wildly unrealistic in your opinion, but please pose them as policy options nonetheless. At the same time, it would not be prudent to overwhelm the decision maker with too many choices. Most people cap the menu of options at five choices.

7. Advantages and disadvantages of each policy option: Write this section from the perspective of the entity that you represent. For clarity, you may present the pros and cons of the options in bullet points or outline format. This may seem like stacking the deck, since some options may have only one advantage and several downsides, but it isn't always that obvious.

8. Your recommendation: After prioritizing the relative pros and cons of the above options, please recommend one option to your employer. Yes, this may require going out on a limb on an extremely complex issue that challenges your ethical instincts. But if you have agreed to advise a particular country, organization, or person, then you will be asked to make a recommendation on their behalf.